Adversity's Child

3 Victims & 4 Female Murderers' Stories of Redemption

BY BETTYE SWEET, M.S.

RoseDog Books
PITTSBURGH, PENNSYLVANIA 15238

RoseDog Books
585 Alpha Drive
Suite 103
Pittsburgh, PA 15238
Visit our website at *www.rosedogbookstore.com*

ISBN: 978-1-6495-7898-3
eISBN: 978-1-6495-7919-5

Table of Contents

Acknowledgements

I was inspired to write this, my fourth book, after participating in a Justice Reform Symposium at the California Institution for Women. But my writing was empowered after reading *The Deepest Well* written by Dr. Nadine Burke Harris. I've also watched her YouTube videos. She is a down-to-earth, insightful, funny, brilliant doctor and writer.

I begin each woman's story with Dr. Burke-Harris' ACE (adverse childhood experiences) questionnaire. Her in-depth studies showed how physical, mental, sexual abuse, neglect, mental illness, drug and alcohol addicted parents and also divorce can have long-lasting effects on a person's health, their propensity for drugs and alcohol which often leads to a life of crime, resulting in death or prison. This questionnaire should be in the records of every psychologist, therapist, doctor, nurse, school and hospital for each of their patients. Thank you, Dr. Burke-Harris for this invaluable contribution to American society.

To my daughter, Crystal Philips and my niece, Robin Sweet-Ransom, I thank you two for always being ready to lend an ear to my ideas and projects. A special thanks to one of my best friends, George Bowden, for his support and editing prowess. Also, I'd like to thank Robin for allowing me to include a portion of her story from her book, *Taboo: Untold Family Secrets Revealed.* and a special thank you to Rita DeAnda for sharing her memoirs with me and the world.

Prologue

Aww, the sweet innocence of childhood. We'd like to believe that, wouldn't we? Just like we believed in that big fat, bearded white man whose reindeer-drawn sleigh brought him to your rooftop and who slid down the chimney, leaving you presents once a year. What child hasn't been monetarily rewarded by the tooth fairy for placing a tooth under his or her pillow? What about the Easter bunny?

The sad truth is that they are all made-up stories and many children do not find out the "real deal" until years later. And that's okay because it's all positive, like fairy tales with happy endings. Adverse childhood experiences are negative and imprinted from birth. Millions of children in America have experienced childhood hardships. Many of them have overcome and even transcended these challenges like the Horatio-Alger-like stories.

But what about the children who grow up and their toxic-stressed childhood experiences manifests themselves in negative ways such as alcohol and drug abuse, sexual deprivation, cyclical violence, incest, incarceration, health problems, obesity, and murder? The stories of the seven women highlighted in this book exemplify the potential fall-out of ACE (childhood adverse experiences).

•   •   •   •   •

Ace Survey

The *Deepest Well* by Dr. Burke Harris had a crucial questionnaire (ACE – adverse childhood experiences) that I include at the beginning of each of the seven ladies' stories. Below are the 10 adversities seen in the categories below which happens before the age of eighteen:

1. Emotional abuse (recurrent)
2. Physical abuse (recurrent)
3. Sexual abuse (contact)
4. Physical neglect
5. Emotional neglect
6. Substance abuse in the household – drugs/alcohol
7. Mental illness in the household such as depression
8. Mother treated violently
9. Divorce or parental separation

10. Criminal behavior in household such as someone going to jail

According to Harris, other factors that increases toxic stress risks are homelessness (a huge problem in L.A. and San Francisco), community and police violence, racism, bullying, illness and chronic pain, growing up in the foster care system, death or loss of a caregiver, youth incarceration and abuse from a boyfriend or girlfriend.

•   •   •   •   •

We all know that adversity, tragedy and hardship are a part of life. For the lesser evolved persons or so-called "weak-minded", we know full well about the resultant fall-outs: substance abuse, cyclical violence, incarceration, and health problems. As previously mentioned, you will journey with seven ACE females – three victims and four murderers.

Statistics have shown that 87% of the world's population has experienced at least one ACE score and 49% have an ACE score of 4 or more. It is important that you understand that the ACE score has nothing to do with socio-economic background, religion, education, race, culture, or sexual preference. A person's ACE score – whether it is 1 or 10, has no bearing on the effects of the trauma or adversity.

What makes one person with the same adversities as another travel a different path? I wish I could answer that for you. I'm still trying to figure out me and why I do what I do.

Ch. 1 – BETTYE
Losing My Baby

On December 17, 2004 at 9:35 PM, I was awakened by a loud knocking downstairs. I groggily stumbled down the stairs and opened the door to see two policemen. "What did he do?" I asked.

"He did nothing ma'am. He was shot".

"Shot?" I whispered in disbelief. "Is he dead?"

"No ma'am, but you need to get dressed so we can take you to the hospital."

With trembling hands, I hurriedly dressed. When I returned downstairs, the policeman had gotten off the phone and I could tell by the look on his face that I was about to hear some bad news.

"He didn't make it".

"He didn't make what?" I yelled in disbelief.

"He's dead, ma.am."

I fell to my knees, clutching my chest in agony as I slowly crawled to the bathroom to throw up yellow-greenish, sickening bile. The pain was so excruciating that my spirit left my body and I watched me from above.

Just a week before Christmas and my whole world was forever changed. Jason was my 18 – year old son - a beautiful young man with a loving and generous heart. He was robbed of $500 and shot in the chest. What's a grieving mother to do?

Well, I can't speak for anyone else but myself. I did what I had to do to try to quell this trauma and pain. After the funeral and all the company had died down, I began my journaling journey. Months later, as I re-read them, I noticed the strategies or steps that I'd taken on my journey toward peace. This discovery morphed into my third book: *Survivor to Thriver – A Mother's Journey Toward Peace After Her Son's Murder.* I know, it's a long title but it says it all.

•　　•　　•　　•　　•

Writing allows you to get everything out – good and bad – on paper in black and white. The seven strategies toward healing that I identified in my book morphed into a ten week *Write to Heal Program* – a one-hour weekly pull-out program for secondary school children with PTSD.

The other thing that was crucial to my healing was attending support groups with grieving mothers like myself. I joined about six or seven groups, desperately seeking peace. Through my association with Justice for Murdered Children, I was privileged to meet Rebecca Weicker, CEO and founder of Justice Reform.

I was intrigued with her prison reform program and couldn't wait until I was cleared so I could see what it was like to enter a prison as a provider instead of as an inmate's visitor. Plus, I wanted to further my connections and resources for my Free 4 Lyfe re-entry program for ex-offenders.

After my clearance, I was involved in a Transformative Justice Symposium at the California Institution for Women in Corona, California. It was a two-day event re: Healing from Violence: Exploring Trauma & Resilience. It was one of the most amazing experiences of my life. There were 20 survivors, 40 inmates, and 20 people from the DA's office, judges, wardens, commissioners, mental health providers – 80 people in total. We were put in groups of 10. There were four inmates in my group. They all were murderers.

We sat in circles and each person was allotted a certain amount of time for each of the six prompts which were:

Introduce yourself and tell us why you're here;

Survivors: Please share the name of your loved one and how long since their murder?

Inmates: Please share how long you've been incarcerated, your sentence, your conviction and name of victim. 1 minute

Survivors: Please tell us who your loved one was and who you were before they died.

Inmates: what were some life experiences that contributed to who you were before your crime? 7-8 minutes

Survivors: Since your loved one died, what are some of the barriers in your healing journey and what was a pivotal moment towards healing?

Inmates: Since the commission of your crime, what have been the barriers in your healing and the pivotal moment towards your healing? 7-8 minutes

Survivors: What has been your greatest source of strength since your loved one died?

Inmates: What has been your greatest source of strength since your incarceration? 3-5 minutes

Both: What have you learned today that was new for you? How will you take care of yourself after today?

These prompts incited such honest and poignant heart-felt responses that everyone was reaching for the box of Kleenex in the middle of the circle. I wish I had stock in Kleenex. Every circle was experiencing the same raw emotions as our group. The empathy that I felt for these "murderers" was overwhelming. I felt their pain and remorse. I kissed and hugged each of them as we sobbed together.

I drove home that first day with their stories bombarding my senses. I went to bed with them on my mind. What could I do to help bring peace to these women? The next day I had it! I told them to begin journaling, starting with meeting me at the symposium. Next, they were to go back to their childhood and tell their story of their life experiences that led them to prison. I had obsessed on a number of titles and finally settled on, *Adversity's Child- 3 Victims &4 Female Murderers' Stories of Redemption*.

My friend, Sherry B., had recommended a must-read book. *The Deepest Well* by Dr. Nadine Burke Harris turned out to be one of the most enlightening, eye-opening books about the long-term effects of childhood adversity that I've ever read.

When I got to the third chapter, I was surprised at the floodgate of tears washing down my face as her words jolted me back to my four-year old self. Now, I had to share my story. Maybe it could further my healing.

• • • • •

CH. 2 – BETTYE
My Childhood

Because of my Christian upbringing with my God-loving parents and the emotional and spiritual support I was given, my self-esteem was intact. I can hear my mother's voice ringing in my ear (God rest her soul), "That girl is smart as a whip". I was the first born and a natural leader.

I went to elementary school at Pecan Grove, a school built in the middle of a pecan grove. At recess, we'd pelt other kids with pecans or gorge ourselves with them. I was one of five Negro children there. Everyone else was white. Their only Black employee was the janitor, father of one of the students. Because my reading level was well above everyone else (I was reading the Bible at five), I was skipped to the third grade the following year. Being smarter than all of the other kids added to my air of confidence.

Growing up with "unconditional love" and always being ahead of my classmates, further fostered my sense of well-being and self-assurance. I believe that is why I refused to put up with too much crap. Like I've said before, "Three strikes and you're out". I never married anyone who I loved *and* respected. That's how I could leave without a backwards glance. They never deserved me anyway.

I grew up knowing what true love and commitment was all about. It was no secret that my father was crazy about our mother. He loved and respected her and would let any and everyone know that. He was the provider and protector. He was handsome and strong. He didn't lie, steal, or cheat. He was a man after God's own heart and mine.

•　　•　　•　　•　　•

Number 3 was my only ACE number. I remember.my Uncle Mack, pastor and husband of my mom's sister, Aunt Lena, starting out with placing me on his lap. I could feel myself slowing levitating as his penis became more engorged as he held me by my waist.

He would later, take out his penis and place my little hands on it. I was fascinated with how big I could make it grow. Then, came the squirting of that white stuff that we all know now, as semen or the more common term, cum. I knew that it was wrong what he was doing, but then I also enjoyed my power with the magic stick.

I didn't tell my parents or anyone else because I knew that it wouldn't end well for Uncle Mack or my father. Even as young as I was, I knew the repercussions if I told, so I subtly blackmailed my uncle into giving me 50 cents each time. I jokingly say that he turned me into a 50 cent four-year-old ho'. That was when sodas cost 10 cents, candy bars, 5 cents and are smaller and cost much more today, and potato chips cost a nickel. You know how many friends I could buy with that?

I'm not trying to minimize the experience. It's just that it is in my DNA to take the victor route rather than the victim. I know for sure had he penetrated or invaded my body it would have been a whole different story and outcome. That's why I have an attitude of gratitude because I wasn't threatened and/or seriously violated.

That being said, there is no excuse for Uncle Mack's actions. I have been blessed not to have any serious emotional, mental or physiological problems as a result of that adverse childhood experience. I had a happy childhood with loving parents and my six siblings.

Maybe Uncle Mack is why I made most men pay when I was in my twenties and thirties. They'd always get off and I wouldn't. So, I had to get something out the deal. Getting paid and receiving expensive gifts worked for me.

So, why were the tears profusely cascading down my cheeks and dripping down my breasts when I got to the third chapter in Dr. Burke-Harris' book? I pondered and wondered about how many of my life experiences and choices were predetermined by this, and the other grown-ass men — uncles, preachers, deacons, and others who I'd learned to fight off. I especially hated when I was subjected to the sexual advances from almost every husband when driving me home after babysitting. I thought, all dicks are tricks except my dad.

• • • • •

Ch. 3 - BETTYE
Serial Monogamist

A person's ACE score – whether it is 1 or 10, has no bearing on the effects of the trauma or adversity. My ACE score of 1 perhaps could be the reason I've had five husbands. After only a few weeks with my psychologist, I realized that I had, what I coined a, "Zeus Complex." That's when you think you can save the world or in my case, my husbands.

When I was a teacher at Jefferson High School, we had a guest poetry teacher speak to my students. I felt sorry for her when she told us she'd never had both love and respect at the same time for any of her men. In my rumination, I discovered I was just like her. I'd loved many men but the Aussie was the one who came closest to being loved and respected by me.

I married my first husband at the tender age of 17. Lee was my first love. He was the football captain at

Lincoln High School in San Diego. Not only was he a great athlete, he had a voice on him and boy, could be croon! Although he was a mere 5'9" (I prefer taller men), he won me over with his confident, gregarious personality. He was sporting a process which was popular with the 60's cool cats. My dad didn't like that. For those of you who don't know what a process is, it's a perm to straighten your hair, then it gets waved.

Having fathered four girls, my father was very strict and protective. I never went out on dates or partied like everyone else because it was a "sin". I could, however, make money by babysitting. I'd take care of my duties, put the kids to bed and call Lee. I did it only once and ended up getting pregnant and married five months later.

Hearing all my life, "As long as you are under my roof, you will abide by my rules", I couldn't wait to be out from under his roof – great for me but bad for my husband who found me a little hard to handle. I'm sure he grew weary of my mantra: "You're not my father – you can't tell me what to do."

It was no surprise that we broke up when our daughter was about six months old. I packed my things, took our daughter to my parents with promises of coming to get her after getting settled in Los Angeles and left San Diego and my childhood without so much as a backward glance.

I was a great long-distance mom. I never missed birthdays or holidays and my parents were even better parents to her than I would've been. When I got it together months later and came to get my daughter, my mother told me it would break her heart if I took her away.

•   •   •   •   •

I wouldn't marry again until twenty years later. I was off living my best life – having a good time. My daughter was happy with my parents, I was traveling all across the U.S. and Europe singing background for Gary Wright, Ann-Margret, and Cuba Gooding, Sr. I performed with a four-girl group called the Delicates, entertaining American troops in Thailand, China and Japan. I was cast in three movies and traveled first class promoting them. I even sang in the White House with Ann-Margret during the Ford administration. I was living the life of a starlet, secure with the knowledge that my daughter was well cared for with my parents.

Twenty years later, I decided that I was ready for a son. I got pregnant but didn't want to marry my baby's daddy. Instead, I married Stuart, an Aussie from Sydney who was working as a telemarketer with my boyfriend at the time.

John was his name. he went vacationing in the Philippines and came back with too many sex stories. Afraid of catching some foreign sexual disease, I decided to dump him and started dating Stuart who had developed a wonderful relationship with my son. As a matter of fact, when we got married, three-year old Jason gave me away. That was the cutest thing.

We remained married for about three years before I divorced him because he had gotten into some type of trouble and had to return to Sydney. We have remained friends over the years, though. He is currently remarried to a lovely lady who has two sons from a previous marriage. That's the saga of husband #2.

• • • • •

I met my third husband while Stuart and I were doing outreach to the homeless in downtown Los Angeles with our church. Jesse was a tall, good-looking man, well-mannered and intelligent. He impressed us so much that we took him home to help with taking my son to school, to help with cleaning and cooking. He was a big help to this working mother who was also taking college night classes.

After Stuart and I broke up, we slowly developed a relationship. He was awfully handy around the house –

fixing the roof and helping with the landscaping. I got him a job and he was able to help with the bills and a good lover. He was great with my son. He had potential.

My advice: Encourage and help people with potential – just don't marry them. After two years of marriage, we had a Halloween party. He got drunk, we had an argument, and he laid hands on me! That is a mortal no no!

The next day, which was the Rodney King riot, he went to work and by the time he was able to make it back home, Jason and I had moved, leaving him with two weeks paid rent, a bed, towels, a skillet, a pan, two plates, two spoons, two forks, and two knives. He didn't know where I'd laid my last steps. I filed my own divorce papers, like before. The first time it cost $35 to file in 1967. In 2013, the cost had risen to $350.

•　　•　　•　　•　　•

My fourth marriage was to this handsome, tall, karate black belt instructor. He is the only man who could always satisfy my sexual appetite. He was perfect in every way except he was addicted to heroin and other drugs. I decided that I could fix him if I married him. I had great Kaiser insurance. He went to rehab and I knew life would be perfect after that. Not!!

We went through four years of rehab, remission, rehab, remission until finally I got tired of hiding my jewelry and sleeping with my money nestled in my bra. Even though I'd have to forfeit the awesomest (I know it's not a word) sex ever, I had to do it. That was my fourth divorce.

•　　•　　•　　•　　•

I met my last husband early 2011. I was immediately stricken by this 6'4", 280-pound, handsome hunk of a man. I met him while driving home from my school. He lived in Temecula and invited me out. I went and had the best time. He was a big spender. He had a lot of rich, influential friends. He had his own business and was living in a 3-bedroom condo.

The thing that stuck out most was the ten or fifteen pictures he had placed all around the place of his son. You would've thought he was dead. When I inquired, I was told simply, that they no longer had a rapport since his divorce.

I decided then and there that we'd never be fully happy unless he could rekindle his relationship with his son. I set out to do just that. His ex-wife and I became fast friends and I was able to work the family back together again. But then I found out that the son and the mother had opioid addictions and that was what started the demise of our marriage.

My last husband allowed his drugged-out son and his son's girlfriend to drive us apart. He'd rather listen to his son rather than my good sensible recommendations. He stole from both of us and was always defended by his father. I got tired of that, among other things like being accused of cheating. After seven years of love and challenges, I left him too. We've tried that friendship thing but it's not working because my ex still envisions us getting back together again. I will always love him but without deep counseling, he is no good for me or anyone else.

•　　•　　•　　•　　•

Yes, I thought my ACE number 3 was the reason for much of my life experiences because of the sexual molestation that began at the tender age of four. But after my psychological evaluations, I found out that wasn't really the case or was it?

My visit to CIW opened my eyes to a lot of things. The main thing was the number of ACEs I saw as I listened to each one's story. I was blessed with "perfect" parents. None of the women in our circle had that. Some of the abuse that they suffered at the hands of their own biological parents was heartbreaking.

"Except for the grace of God, there go I" was a familiar saying when I was growing up. I've done things that could have landed me behind bars. I remember driving Rosie, an old dope dealer, to Vegas for a drug drop-off in 1988.

We made sure that everything was mechanically right with the car. We'd heard of people getting busted just because they were stopped for not having brake lights. I made sure that I never exceeded the posted speed signs.

We were met by two ladies in nurse uniforms in the back of the motel where we discreetly exchanged the pounds of cocaine for dollar bills. I received $500 for driving. The money that I made for this excursion would have paled in comparison to the time I would have served had I got caught. I'm not proud of that. I must have really needed the money. I dodged that bullet.

Although I escaped being arrested that time, I have been arrested four times. The first time was when I first moved to Los Angeles. I was nineteen. I'd met this beautiful young girl, Trina, who introduced me to her "man" who offered me a job working in his massage parlor.

I found out later that he was a pimp and Trina was one of his "ladies". I was taught how to do a proper massage and for an extra $10, guys could get jerked off. I didn't need lessons for that. My Uncle Mack had taught me that when I was four.

I had worked there for about a week and a half when I had my first arrest. What happened was I walked into the room and this well-built, towel-clad young man was lying on his stomach. We exchanged formalities and I drizzled lotion on his back and began the massage. All of a sudden, he jumped up and announced that he was a policeman and that I was under arrest!

I was looking far too cute in my pink uniform to be sitting in the back seat of a police car. While behind bars, a parade of policemen was walking by, checking me out and making comments. I was booked and released because there were no charges. The rookie policeman had acted too soon.

My second arrest happened when I was living in Encino with my girlfriend. At the time I didn't know she was addicted to heroin. That's why now I believe it was easy for me to talk her into writing bad checks to the White Front chain. Years ago, this was like today's Cosco or Walmart. "You're white and you can get away with it. Just report your checks stolen and get to writing". She did.

We went on a check-writing shopping spree. We got televisions, fur coats, jewelry – anything that could be fenced. There was this hump-backed friend of mine named Andre who was supposed to buy the stuff from us. But instead, he and two of his "boys" came one night, pointed a gun at my head and took everything and didn't give us a dime!

Two days later, we both were arrested in front of our neighbors and taken to jail. We were put in the same cell. We were scared as hell and she started being sick. Luckily someone bailed her out and I was released shortly after that because they had nothing on me.

My third arrest happened while living in Huntington Beach and coming from a nightclub in Los Angeles. While on the freeway, I was changing the radio station when my car swerved a little. I was immediately pulled over, failed the sobriety walk test and was taken to the station in Simi Valley. I passed the blood alcohol level test and they had to return me to my car. That was scary!

My fourth and final arrest, I hope, happened when my daughter and I were driving from a prison near Yuma where we'd visited one of my grandsons. As we approached the check point, we saw a long line of cars. When we finally made it to the front of the line, we saw a little white dog, sniffing tires. When he got to our rental car, he stopped and a policeman motioned us to pull over.

My daughter pulled over as instructed and I nervously pulled out my weed card to show them that the gram I had was legal. But not so with the Feds. I was handcuffed and booked while my car was being searched. People were driving by looking at me and pointing — the handcuffed criminal. It was cold. Melting snow was on the side of the road. I didn't know if I was shivering from the cold, fear or embarrassment.

Three hours later, my daughter and I finally got back on the road. We both rejoiced after finding the roach that they failed to find when they searched the car. We needed a smoke.

These arrests might seem minor to some people and yes, I've had some lucky breaks. But being an ordinary citizen, those arrests were traumatic to me. I can not imagine what the women felt when they received their verdict — when the judge said, "I sentence you to 25 to life."

All of the women that I write about in this book are overcomers. I begin with Anna Mae Bullock because she's one of the pioneers of overcomers.

•　　•　　•　　•　　•

CH. 4– OVERCOMERS
Anna Mae

I have always been an avid reader. The first book I read was the Bible. I was five. I didn't start writing until I became an adult. I'm sure I did a little writing in high school but most of my writing happened during my college years. Writing and journaling is an art form that I hope lives on forever. Writing got me through the darkest moments of my life.

I've read many books about people who have overcome childhood adversity. Many of the fallouts from these atrocities were substance abuse, cyclical violence, incarceration, alcoholism, and mental and physical health problems. But what makes some people fall victim and succumb to these problems while others seem to rise above it?

What doesn't kill you, could heal you. There are many stories of people facing unsurmountable challenges and hardships who have lived to overcome and even surpass ordinary circumstances.

I applaud the resilience and the tenacity of all ACE survivors. One of the people that I have loved and admired all my life is Tina Turner.

Anna Mae Bullock was born on November 26, 1939, in Nutbush, Tennessee. Her parents, Floyd and Zelma Bullock were poor sharecroppers who, early in her life, split up and left the two sisters to be raised by their grandmother. When the grandmother died in the early 1950's, the two sisters moved to St. Louis, Missouri to be with their mother.

This woman is one of my sheroes for sure. She had an ACE score of 8 out of 10 but still rose above all of those adversities. Anna Mae had a painful childhood. There was addiction and violence all around her growing up. Because of these childhood adversities, she struggled in school, as do most traumatized children.

Why didn't she succumb to drugs and alcohol? I believe that it was her talent and finding someone who believed in her. Her abusive husband, Ike Turner, gave her a career, a family, beatings, and disrespect. She finally had the strength to leave him and resurrect her career on her own terms.

I really admire her because she took all of the steps to walk out of devastating circumstances and into the light. Meeting her much younger husband, Erwin, and marrying him was a super positive move and at the right time.

Your ACEs may not manifest itself through alcoholism, drug and other addictions, unwise choices or criminal behavior but it can affect your immune system, your body and your mind over time.

That's what happened to Tina Turner. She escaped all of the above pitfalls but her body is paying for the trip. Right after her honeymoon with her dream man, she had a stroke and had to learn to walk again; after that, she found out she had intestinal cancer and then, kidney failure!

Nothing gets you through anything like a strong support system. Her new husband was just that. He gave her one of his kidneys and has been by her side since then. He was there to comfort her when her son committed suicide. She is in her eighties now. I saw a recent picture of her. Girlfriend still looks good! I'm always pleased when people compare me to Ms. Tina although we're ten years apart.

What makes people with the same ACE scores go into different directions? Some become drug-addicted, some abuse alcohol, others engage in unlawful activities and some end up with serious sexual deviate behaviors. Incarceration or an early death are the most likely end results.

I am not only a survivor, I'm a thriver. Hearing the stories of how childhood adversities shapes lives makes me appreciative of my early beginnings. My strong support base also helped me to do the hardest thing I've ever done and that is forgiving my son's murderer.

Forgiveness doesn't mean that you have to forget what happened. It doesn't mean that you don't stop working hard as you can to do everything that you can do to get the killer incarcerated and doing time.

Why is it that I can forgive my son's murderer but not Uncle Mack, my childhood molester? I realize now that it's because David was remorseful and begged my forgiveness but not that serial pedophile uncle/preacher of mine.

Each one of the seven ladies highlighted in this book has had to forgive and four of them are seeking forgiveness – even begging for it because forgiving cleanses the soul, boosts your immune system and lowers blood pressure.

• • • • •

CH. 5 – ROBIN

Stop Abusing My Mother

My niece, Robin, who authored a book about incest had an ACE score of 4 - #3, #6, #7, #8 (see ACE Survey). This is her story:

• • • • •

Like many people, I came from a broken home. In November, 1969, my parents married when my mother, Sheila Denise, was seventeen and my father, Darrell Wayne, was eighteen. My father was my mother's first boyfriend and they were madly in love. Unfortunately, they were forced to marry because my maternal grandmother discovered that they were having sex and this infuriated her. She told my mother that either they marry or she'd put her in juvenile hall. For some reason they believed her threats and got married.

A few months into their teen marriage, my mother got pregnant and I was born in January, 1971. My sister showed up in October, 1973. Later, my parents decided that they couldn't make a "go" of marriage and separated.

My mother was a beautiful woman and thus had countless admirers. Some became live-in boyfriends. She had a relationship with a man I detested. When he was home, I tried not to be. I used to love to stare at him with my moon-sized dark eyes while sucking my right thumb and folding my left ear. I used to pretend that I had secret powers and that if I stared at him long enough, he'd die! It brings back a chuckle when I think of my five-year-old fantasy. However, he didn't think it was funny. He used to hate when I did that. It was like he could read my murderous thoughts towards him. Every now and then, he'd ask my mama to make me stop. I would for a few minutes and then I'd start up again.

My mother had our downstairs manager baby-sit me after school. I loved it down there. They were a blended family. The husband was a preacher with two teenaged sons from a previous relationship. They were fourteen and fifteen. He and his wife had a three-year-old son to-gether. The younger of the teenaged boys had my first name, so to avoid confusion, they called me by my middle name, Latrice.

Since I loved it down there and I was the only girl, I began spending full weeks and weekends with them. I was like their very own daughter. I cherished that position in their family.

Their oldest boy knew that I loved to talk. One time I told him about the fact that I'd heard my mother and her boyfriend making strange noises in their bedroom. He later blackmailed me with that information. I believed that if he told my mama that I was telling her business that she'd spank me and stop me from spending so much time downstairs and I dreaded that. Even though I missed sleeping in the same room with my two-year-old sister, I didn't want to be in the same house as my mother's abusive boyfriend.

One time, he was beating my mother. It got so bad that he straddled her on the floor and began to choke her. There was also a time when he kicked her with his steel-toed work boots. On the latter occasion when he was choking her, I'd had enough! I was only five but I knew I had to do something to get this animal off my mother. After all, if he killed her, who would take care of my sister and me?

I marched into the kitchen and picked up a huge chef's knife. I went back into the living room and stood over him. I said: "Get off of my mama now before I kill you!" He looked up and he couldn't believe his eyes.

Here was this pint-sized little girl standing over him ready to cut him from A to Z. I'm sure he had flashbacks of all the times I stared at him with murderous intent.

He asked my mother to tell me to put the knife down. "Not until you get off of her." He immediately obeyed me and only then did I return the knife to its place. I could tell that my mother was impressed yet fearful of my display of bravery. I'm sure she knew how ugly it could've gotten and that most likely we both could have been killed by him, but she admired my guts and love for her.

Hell, I didn't know that he could kill us. At that point, I thought I was "Super Robin" and nothing would keep me from defending my mother and killing that jackass! I never saw him hit her again after that. So now you can see where the idea was birthed in me that it's my duty to protect victims and underdogs. I still feel that way and make no apologies for it, although now, I choose more effective means than violence.

• • • • •

CH. 6 – ROBIN
Sexual Molestation

I digress. Let me get back to this boy. So, one afternoon after he'd come from school, his stepmother left us alone in the apartment. He brought me into his room and turned on some music and said that we were going to play a game. The game involved me "dancing" while lying on my back on his bed. Sounded like fun to me and he knew how much I loved to dance. I knew all the new dances and thought this was a new one I needed to learn. I couldn't wait!

So, I got on his bed and tried to "dance". He then surprised me and lay on top of me. He said that he was "dancing" too as he rocked on me back & forth. He tickled me a bit and I laughed. I thought it was a game. What did I know? He never took off his clothes or mine and never touched my vagina with his hands, so I didn't initially think there was anything wrong with it. After all, I was only five and he was fifteen. I guess this went on for a couple months or so when we were alone.

I recall one time when one of his friends rang the doorbell. He didn't let the boy in and rushed back to me. I asked him to let his friend join us and he said no and reminded me that I couldn't tell anyone or he'd tell my mother what I told him about the noises she made in her room. It was then that I became uncomfortable and thought that something was wrong since he threatened me. I stopped cooperating and it stopped as suddenly as it began.

I wish I could say that was my only encounter with being molested, but it wasn't. It would become less playful and more brutal.

• • • • •

CH. 7 – ROBIN
Lester, the Molester

My mother eventually left that low-life boyfriend of hers and we moved to another city and apartment. It felt good to live in a house with just my sister, my mother and me. We could walk around scantily clothed and not be concerned about an abusive man trying to call the shots.

When I was nine, my mother met Lester. They met at a house party and it was "love at first sight" for them. My sister and I really liked him a lot. He was handsome. At the time, Jheri curls were in and his was thick, full and shoulder length. He was 5'11 and solidly built. My mom was only 5'2 and he towered over her.

Soon after they got together, my mother got pregnant. I was ecstatic and so was Lester! I'd been praying for another sibling – I didn't care if it was a boy or girl. I just wanted a baby to take care of. Ever since I was 7,

I took care of the neighborhood kids and wanted a baby of my own, so to speak.

Even though Lester didn't move in, he was always at our home, the Pendletons in South Gate. He worked at a department store and showered my mom with gifts for the baby – from clothes to a bassinet and crib. He didn't leave Miko, my sister, and me out. He bought us a new wardrobe of clothes and our first 13-inch color TV to put in our room! That was big stuff in the early eighties! He also bought all the latest albums and my house became the hang out for my booty-shaking friends. I loved to teach new dance steps and since we had one of the best stereos and music in the complex, my house was the place to practice. As you can see, Lester was a wonderful man and for the first time in my life, I actually wanted my mother to be married to someone other than my father.

Tiffani Reshaun was born premature in March, 1981. She was actually due on April 19, (Resurrection Sunday that year). Tiffani was born with jaundice and only weighed a little over four pounds. She couldn't leave the hospital until she weighed five pounds. It was a very stressful time for my mom and me. It broke my mother's heart to have to leave my sister in the hospital. However, the day after my mother had the baby, something interesting happened.

My stepfather and I came home from the hospital to get some clothes to take back to my mother for when she came home. She had a cesarean section and had to stay in the hospital for three to five days. After we'd gotten the clothes, he pulled me down on my mother's bed and began to tickle me. He rolled me over onto my back and he lay on me and continued to tickle me. It was fun. Not surprisingly, I didn't think of the game that boy played with me when I was five. I was ten now.

It wasn't until many years later that I compared the two incidents. Thus, I didn't immediately feel uncomfortable till I got tired of laughing. He got up and we proceeded to leave. That was the first time that he'd ever gotten that physical with me and I just thought he was excited about having a baby girl of his own. He had two other boys that were younger than me and he really wanted a girl.

I was on "cloud 9" when Tiffani finally came home! I loved her so very much. She was caramel-colored with straight, fine, black hair. She was so tiny and always smelled so good. My mother and I took good care of her. We even insisted that people wear a cloth diaper over their face when they held her when she first came home since she was very susceptible to getting sick.

• • • • •

CH 8 – ROBIN
Losing My Baby

I noticed that Tiffani didn't seem as alert as other babies. Remember, I was always taking care of other people's babies and toddlers and prided myself on knowing how to care for them like a grown up. Nowadays, you don't let seven-year-olds take care of babies alone in the house, but back then people trusted me with their kids and would pay me a small stipend.

I began testing Tiff-Tiff's reflexes. She rarely blinked. Most people blink several times in a minute. She didn't. It seemed like it would take a couple minutes or more before she blinked. Another thing that seemed strange is that when I put my hand over her nose and mouth, she wouldn't fight my hand, kick and try to breathe without obstruction. I tested this other baby I baby-sat and she immediately tried to knock my hand away from her face. Granted, she was about one or so, but nevertheless, I felt that Tiff should have responded rather than just lay there as if her breathing wasn't obstructed.

I told my mother about my observations and she told me not to worry about it. She was premature and would catch up. I thought she was right. Tiffani began to gain weight and seemed much livelier. She was getting so cute and I thanked God for giving me a baby sister to take care of. I rushed home every day just to hold my baby.

Tiffani caught a cold and my mother took her to the doctor on a Thursday morning. The doctor told my mother that Tiff-Tiff was fine. He also told my mother to stop letting Tiffani sleep with her. After her early AM feeding, she was to be put in the bassinet that was next to my mother's bed. Up to this point, my mother regularly let Tiffani sleep on her chest or lay next to her after she woke up around 4 AM for her feeding.

The next morning, it was a Friday; my mother woke up around 7 AM and came into my room to wake Miko and me up. She then went back to her room and called for Tiff-Tiff to wake up. Back in those days, doctors told parents to let babies sleep on their stomachs to avoid choking or whatever. So that's how Tiff was sleeping. Usually, Tiff would wake up before we did but this time she didn't respond to my mother's voice.

My mother picked her up and she noticed that mucous was coming out of her mouth and nose and her skin looked greenish and she wasn't breathing. My mother screamed and dropped Tiffani back in the bassinet. I ran into the room and immediately picked up my baby. I cradled her in my arms and begged Jehovah not to let my baby die. Sadly, none of us knew CPR. My mother called her best friend and my grandmother. Someone called the ambulance.

When they arrived, they took Tiffani from me and put something over her face and tried to resuscitate her. I remember seeing her little gowned body jerk in the muscular arm of the EMT who held her as he walked her to the ambulance.

On the way to the hospital, I began to bargain with Jehovah. "Jehovah, if you save my baby sister, I will always serve you. If someone just has to die, take me. She's an innocent baby that has never done anything to anyone. However, at times I can be a bad little girl. Take me instead but spare her. If you don't spare her, I will curse you and tell everyone else to never serve you because you're no good." That was a desperate place and some desperate words for a ten-year-old to utter to her Creator.

When we got to St. Francis Hospital, which incidentally was the hospital I was born in ten years before, I was hopeful that Tiffani would survive. After all, God and I had a deal, right? God answered my prayers and blessed my mom to get pregnant, so certainly he would hear my most recent plea.

The family began to gather in this small waiting room that was set aside for us. Lester comforted my mother as she blamed herself for listening to the doctor and not letting Tiffani sleep with her earlier in the morning when she cried to be held after her feeding. I was blaming that lousy doctor too and declared that we should sue him if my sister died.

After being in the waiting room for about an hour or two, a doctor or nurse came in and said, "We were able to get a heartbeat but couldn't save it. We're sorry that we couldn't save her. Would you like me to bring her in here so that you all can hold her one last time?"

Just typing those words above and recalling them in my head, still brings back the tears although it's been over thirty years since it happened. My sister died from SIDS. She was seven-weeks-old. It was May, 1981.

A few of us took turns holding Tiffani. I held her the longest. *That was my baby*. How could she be gone already? I LOVED her so much and couldn't believe that my time with her was over. I was hurt, outraged and felt betrayed by the doctors and God. How could they let her die? How could they?

I was my mother's right arm. I went with her to pick out the coffin, helped her pick out the clothes and whatever else she needed me to do. Yet no matter how much I tried to be there for my mother, it wasn't enough. My mother fell completely apart. I believe she had a nervous breakdown although she was never hospitalized. A few weeks after the death, I heard her tell her friend that she wished that Miko or I had died instead of Tiffani. I also think she felt that Lester would leave her because she believed he secretly blamed her for Tiffani's death. Hearing those words from my mother, tore Miko and me apart. I began to resent my mother.

●　　●　　●　　●　　●

CH. 9 – ROBIN
My Stepfather, my Abuser

After the death, Lester moved in. He was thoroughly depressed. He started using PCP all the time. He wasn't the same person, but then none of us were. We missed Tiffani so much.

I then made good on my threat to Jehovah. I cursed him out as soon as I came home from the hospital that fateful day. I called him every name in the book and vowed to never serve him again and also vowed to tell others not to have anything to do with him. My sister did whatever I told her to do and followed my example. Knowing this, I told her that we weren't going to be praying to Jehovah anymore. What did it benefit us?

I remember someone telling me that the reason Tiffani died was because God needed a beautiful new flower in his garden. What?!? What kind of sense does that make? I think that's one of the worst things you can say to someone when they lose a loved one. How is it that God (who has everything) needs our loved ones in heaven? Give me a break! That paves the way for people to blame him and become bitter. It's not God's fault that we have sin and death. It's Satan's and Adam & Eve's. Let's lay the blame where it belongs and try to make sense of it another way besides saying God caused it. That type of reasoning made it easier for me to hate Jehovah, thus making me vulnerable and an open target for Satan and his demons.

I remember some of the words Lester used when he began abusing me. I believe we were the only ones in the house and we were in the living room. I was on my way to my room and he was sitting down. He pulled me to him and sat me on his lap and said, "You know I love you very much, right?" I nodded my head.

"I love you like you are my own daughter. Now that I don't have a daughter anymore, the love I was going to give to her, I have to give to you. Do you love me?" I again nodded yes.

"Good because I love you too. I know you miss your daddy, don't you?" I nodded again.

"I know you do. You know since your daddy is not here and my daughter is not here, we're going to have to love each other the way daddies and daughters love one another." With that, he kissed me on my lips, paused, looked into my eyes for my bewildered response, and kissed me again, while rubbing my behind.

I got nervous and stood up. He told me, "Don't be afraid. This is what your daddy would do if he was here. Doesn't your daddy kiss you on the lips?"

He did but it didn't feel the way Lester just made me feel. I felt yucky and quickly went into my room, closed the door and lay on my bed.

The next time he kissed me, he reminded me that it was just a "daddy kiss". Now Lester had kissed me before, but never on the lips and I just didn't understand why he was choosing to do so now. I wondered: Is he telling me the truth? Is he really just showing me "daddy affection?"

•   •   •   •   •

My mother and father weren't speaking at this time; so consequently, she didn't allow him to speak to my sister and me. He lived in San Diego and I don't know when the last time had been since we'd seen him. So, I didn't have him to turn to and ask about this "daddy thing". I thought about asking my mother, but she was so preoccupied with Tiffani's death and her own issues, that she wasn't really there for me emotionally. Besides, during this time, I really didn't like her that much.

Eventually, Lester began to touch my vagina and promise me gifts for letting him. He told me not to tell my mother and sister because they wouldn't understand and would just get jealous of our "special love". Soon, his "nice" approach became more sinister. When I told him that I wanted to tell my mother or at least ask my friends if their fathers did this, he told me that if I opened my mouth, he'd begin to give his "special daddy love" to Miko. She was only seven and I didn't want him to do this to her. I was her protector and he knew I'd do anything to keep her safe.

He then said that my mother would never believe me because she already thought that I was trying to take him away from her. Later he threatened to kill my sister, my mother and my grandmother – the three people I loved the most outside of my father. So, what did I do? I suffered in tearful silence.

•   •   •   •   •

CH. 10 – ROBIN
Redemption

I finally broke the silence by writing my first book, *Taboo: Untold Family Secrets Revealed.* I suppose that you can think of a number of things that are taboo, but there is one that is probably second on the list only to murdering a family member. What is it? *Incest and child molestation.* The act is so depraved that many don't even want to acknowledge that it exists – let alone happened to them or one of their loved ones. The perpetrators pretend that they're not doing it or that it is a mutually agreed upon act. How ridiculous is that?

When was the last time you've heard a 5-year-old say to her father, brother, etc., *"Hey, let's have sex! I love it when you rub my private parts and make me put your penis in my mouth. Oh, and I really like the way you put the pillow over my head to block the screams that come from you putting your adult sized penis into my infantile vagina. Oh yippee! I can't wait!"*

Sounds ludicrous, doesn't it? Yet that's what these filthy beasts – male and female molesters would have you to believe. The act is consensual. **BULL!!!**

•　　•　　•　　•　　•

The outrage over what happened to me and others in my family and how it put a strangle-hold on our adult lives, has led me to boldly speak out about this taboo subject. I was willing to disclose our family secrets in the hopes that it will help other women and possibly men to heal. What I shared may bring pain and shame to my family, but if I'm able to help one young girl or boy to stop the cycle of abuse, it's worth it.

•　　•　　•　　•　　•

CH. 11 – CHERYL
My Childhood

I have a friend that we'll call Cheryl, who like Robin, had her own childhood dilemma. This woman was one of my colleagues while working at a charter school. She was a lovely lady — bright, smart, and the sweetest lady ever. Out of all the women in this book, Cheryl was the least verbose. I couldn't believe it when she shared her childhood adversities with me.

She had the alarming number of 9 of the 10 ACEs. This is her story:

• • • • •

I am the oldest of four siblings. I had two younger brothers and a baby sister. Our mother was schizophrenic. I didn't know what that meant then, but later learned that schizophrenia was a chronic and severe mental disorder that affected a person's thoughts, feelings, and behavior. It is serious mental disorder in which people interpret reality abnormally.

I learned that depression and social withdrawals were the first signs. I can't ever remember my mother laughing, playing with us, or any of the normal things I saw parents on television doing with their children. Those were fairy-tale families that I would dream about.

We never had company. I never met any of my aunts, uncles or grandparents. The only place we were allowed to go was school and occasionally, the supermarket and the Goodwill store where we got our clothes, although my father made a good living.

The thing that I remember the most and had to work on forgiveness the hardest was the meanness and hostility that she exhibited on mostly me. I don't know why I was the chosen scapegoat; maybe because I was the oldest and the strongest. Any criticism or question that she found threatening, she would react violently either with a torrid of curse words or throwing and breaking things.

She would go for days without bathing, but I was the one who was responsible for getting the younger kids bathed, dressed for school, and fed. I was preparing breakfast and lunch for the family at the tender age of four. The house was always a mess except when my father was expected back home.

My mother was tall and willowy. I thought she was one of the most beautiful women I'd ever seen. Apparently, so did my dad. There was no doubt that he was madly in love with her. Her luxurious blond locks framed her flawless white complexion. She rarely left the house and always kept the drapes drawn. The only sunlight I ever saw was the few times when I was allowed to go to school.

Where was my father and how did he handle the mess of a wife that he married, you might ask? He was a cross-country truck driver for a big company and we only saw him about ten days out of the month. I'm sure he loved his job because it was escape. My mother would take her meds whenever he was around but he has witnessed enough of her episodes, as we called them.

I remember once when my mother answered the phone and someone hung up on her, she got off the phone yelling and throwing things at my father, accusing him of cheating. His adamant denial didn't do anything but fuel the flame. My father was an easy-going laid-back man and he'd do anything to avoid confrontation. He ran out the house and came back with flowers and chocolates (she loved chocolates) and I later heard sounds coming from their bedroom later that night.

My father was a short, stocky man, around 5'8". He had bushy eyebrows and a mustache and a beard. He was a red-headed Irishman – direct contrast to my mom's blonde Swedish good looks. I think he felt lucky to have landed such a beauty and would turn a blind eye to all of her indiscretions.

He was a better husband than he was a father, always bowing down to her wishes and demands. He believed the lies she would tell him about the scars and bruises that bore witness to her abuse. We were never left alone with him to "tell" on her and so we all suffered in silence – most of all, me.

Even though we never got quality time with our father, life was good because we had breakfast and dinner like the families we saw on TV. Mother made our lunches and we went off to school just like normal kids. We dreaded the day that our father would leave. He thought we were crying tears because we were going to miss him – that part was true, but also, we were crying tears of dread. We knew the med-popping would stop and the Mama Dearest would be back.

●　　●　　●　　●　　●

CH. 12 – CHERYL
Out of the Attic

S he's back! My father has gone and soon we'll be
back to our "normal" life of neglect, verbal and
physical abuse. We tip-toed around, trying to be the best
children, trying to do everything right, trying to avoid
the inevitable.

I've been thrown in the attic countless times for the
least little thing. The last one happened just before
my father was scheduled to return home. I had accidently broken a plate which sent my mother into one
of her many rages. It was obvious that she hadn't taken
her meds.

My mother heard the plate crash on the floor and
rushed into the kitchen and grabbed me by my hair and
beat my face into the floor. She busted my nose. Blood
was everywhere. My siblings were huddled together in
the kitchen corner, shaking and crying. They watched

helpless as she made me clean up the mess and dragged me up the stairs to the attic. She threw me in, begging and pleading, then slammed and locked the door.

I lay bruised and bleeding on the cold attic floor. I was surrounded by boxes of books and other household items. I could tell morning from night because of the light shining through the small attic window. I kept my mind occupied by reading the plethora of books housed there. I must have read over a hundred books in my many trips there before my father came home sooner than expected and found me there.

He had arrived home and not seeing me, asked where I was. My baby sister pointed up to the attic. I'd never seen my father that angry before. He scooped me up into his burly, strong arms and cried manly tears. He saw dried-up feces and a couple of fresh piles. The stench was disgusting and putrid.

What happened after that remains a blur. I remember being carried downstairs. I was weak and feeling sick. I hadn't eaten in days. The brother next to me usually would sneak food and water to me but he hadn't been able to do that this time. My father called 911. When the paramedics arrived and saw my condition, they immediately contacted social services.

When I arrived at the hospital, I was rushed to the emergency ward where I was met by the police and a social worker. I was reluctant to share my experiences with them, but the lady officer was very nice and kind and I finally ended up breaking down and telling them my life's story.

•   •   •   •   •

CH. 13 – CHERYL
Redemption

My life changed after that. I remained in the hospital for three days. I was dehydrated and well below the normal weight for a nine-year old. My father was questioned and released and my mother was committed to a mental health facility. We were blessed and lucky to be adopted by the Hamiltons. They had been married for seven years, had two miscarriages and opened their home and heart to four youngsters, ages 9, 8, 6 and 4.

They were the parents we dreamed of having. We missed our father and our mother, but did not miss the trauma and drama. We slowly start becoming normal kids. We were enrolled in the neighborhood public school and because of my advanced reading skills, I quickly caught up to speed with my education and graduated at 17 like I was supposed to.

I worked my way through college and graduated with honors with a BS in Sociology. I was able to get several good-paying jobs and ended up working at YouthBuild, USA, an education and construction program for at-risk youth, ages 16 to 25. I worked there for 15 years.

Five years before I would be retiring, I ran into one my childhood friends. It was Harriet, my best friend all through high school. We had lost touch and it was euphoric running into her again. We exchanged numbers and made plans to meet for dinner that evening.

She caught me up to speed about her life, revealing to me she was gay. I'd been in several heterosexual relationships but was single at the time. We enjoyed several drinks and left the restaurant/bar feeling no pain. Harriet called an Uber and we were driven right to her place.

We tumbled onto her bed and before I knew it, we were kissing and grinding against one another. She deftly undressed me and I had sex with a woman for the first time. It was one of the most pleasurable experiences of my life.

We wasted no time before I moved into her home and we got married a year later. When I retired, we bought and moved into a custom-built home in Stockton, Arizona. I had my first book published – *The Power of Forgiveness* and I've had several successful book signings. I've never been happier.

My only problem is that my sweat glands had been over-exerted as a child and now living in Arizona where the average temperature is 90 degrees, I can't sweat. I think that's a small price to pay for my adverse childhood experiences, don't you agree?

•   •   •   •   •

CH. 14 – CARLA
My Childhood

Carla is one of my many godchildren. She was my colleague Dr. Steve Jefferson's special education student at Jefferson High School. She was also one of the fastest girls on the track team that he coached.

Dr. Jefferson took a special interest in her and would sometimes even track her down and bring her to school. She had serious anger management issues. She was skinny (weighted 105 soaking wet) and wiry and would fight at the drop of a hat and win, as well.

I didn't get to know her until Steve introduced her to me, requesting a position for her at my new charter school for youth 16 to 25 years old. She nervously answered my questions. She told me later that I was questioning her like a drill sergeant. I decided to give her a chance and hired her to be my art instructor, as well as helping her work toward getting her diploma.

She had all ten ACES. Never had I met anyone with so many adverse childhood experiences. Imagine, an ACE score of 10! She was lucky she never did anything to send her to prison. I think that the love for her children is what saved her. Here's her story:

• • • • •

My father left us right after the birth of my baby sister. My mom, who I found out later had been sexually molested by her uncle since the age of four, had been abusing drugs since she was sixteen. Our father was the neighborhood's "pusher man". Being her confidant and best friend, he would make sure that she had what she needed – be it food, bus fare, clothing or drugs.

Of course, no man does all this for a woman without expecting something in return. Their sexual escapades resulted in the birth of five children — three girls and twin boys. My mom's drug use affected us girls more than the boys.

After my father left, her drug use got really bad. We spent the majority of the time with our grandmother and then when our mom was evicted, we all had to crowd into the already over-crowded three-bedroom house full time. My mom would come and go as she pleased, knowing that Grannie would take care of us.

My mom had several "boyfriends" but one stands out more than the others. I think it was because she was so in love with him. He was a handsome devil, I have to admit, but he was a crackhead and a dealer. Every time I'd see him, I knew what time it was – it was high time!

My mom would do anything for him which included letting him have sex with my 12-year old sister. I don't know when or how it started but it finally came to a head when my sister refused to have sex with him anymore. My mother argued with her and the next thing I knew my sister was running out the house with my mom in hot pursuit.

I watched in horror and disbelief at the age of eight as my mom chased my sister, caught her and beat her to death! I had to testify in court against my mom and her family and my siblings turned against me. She was sentenced 25 to life. I was put in a foster home. The abuse I suffered at the hands of my foster caretakers was challenging, to say the least.

Imagine how happy I was when, a year later, I was awarded to my biological father and was allowed to go home. I was now nine- years old, my baby sister was five and my twin brothers were fourteen.

• • • • •

CH. 15 – CARLA
Back Home Again

It was great being home. I quickly assumed the role of mother- cooking, cleaning, and caring for my baby sister. The boys were pretty much on their own – living their best life. They were now being raised by our father after living with granny forever in a three - bedroom house with ten other people.

I grew up with a great love of sports – track and field, basketball, hockey and football. My grandest memories are the family huddling and cuddling on the weathered couch, watching Monday night football. I can still smell the corn popping in the microwave. We learned the hard way not to set the timer to three. There are few things more pleasing to the nostril than fresh popcorn. But even fewer things smell worse than burnt popcorn.

• • • • •

My father had his own maintenance business and we'd all go help clean up office buildings and restaurants. Instead of receiving allowances, we got paid. My brothers received $15 and us girls, $10. The ten dollars I got was enough to cover my wants and needs.

When I turned fourteen, I demanded $20 weekly. My argument was that I did all the cooking and most of the cleaning, as well. My father finally agreed, and the boys received that same salary increase.

From the outside looking in, we looked like a regular normal family. But looks can be deceiving. My father was praised for taking such good care of us four motherless children. He took care of both our needs and his. His needs were sexual gratification from me, his nine-year old daughter. I dreaded coming home from school and finding him getting high. He'd only rape me when he was high. He loved me, he just had his issues, I'd reason.

This continued until I turned sixteen and he was diagnosed with stage four cancer. God don't like ugly. His health quickly declined. My brothers and I had to handle his business. With me taking care of my father, cleaning restaurants and office buildings, cooking and cleaning, I had little time for school.

Mr. Jefferson soon grew tired of my many excuses and me dodging him for not going to school. He finally stopped pushing me to go to school and started helping me navigate through life. He was one of the few men in my life who didn't want sexual favors. He was genuinely a good guy. I could count on him and I shared everything with him except my father's sexual abuse.

I never told anyone, but I think my baby sister knew. I could tell by the way she'd look at me the following morning after one of our love sessions. She ended up with her own issues, thinking that I was prettier than her and that's why my father preferred me to her.

I hate to say this, but I have to admit, I took advantage of my father during his almost one-year struggle with the cancer. I had power of attorney and so I was able to cash his checks. That was the beginning of my alcohol abuse. I was determined not to go down the cracked-out path, like my mom. I figured liquor was a quicker route to escape. I'd get lit and want to fight.

•   •   •   •   •

CH. 16 – CARLA
D-Day

My father wasn't the only man violating my childish body. There was this man who lived in the neighborhood who would always say stuff to me whenever I passed him on my way to school or even going to the neighborhood liquor store. I would scurry past him as fast as I could. He was a creepy grown-ass pedophile.

Late one evening when I was leaving the liquor store, suddenly I felt someone grab me. He covered my mouth with his hand to muffle my screams. I was then dragged into the alley and brutally raped. I was no virgin to sexual abuse, but this wasn't love like with my father. This was really rape I thought, as I struggled unsuccessfully beneath him on the dirt alley floor. He warned me if I told anyone he'd kill me and my baby sister, so I kept quiet.

I didn't know his name then but I knew who he was – the pedophile who was always hitting on me. That incident would be the first of many. Remember, I'm a fighter, so I decided that I would start carrying a knife and that I'd fuck him up the next time he raped me.

I'll never forget that day. It was nightfall and I was just about to enter the liquor store when I saw him. I took off running into the alley with him in hot pursuit. I could smell the mixture of cheap cologne and liquor as he caught up with me and threw me to the ground. But I was ready for his ass this time.

I plunged the knife as hard as I could into his heart. He fell on top of me and I struggled to get from underneath him. He was easily twice my weight. I looked down and saw that his blood was all over me.

I don't remember anything more except collapsing on the living room floor, covered in blood, crying and screaming uncontrollably. As usual, only my baby sister and father were there. She was hollering, not knowing what to do – afraid for her big sister. My father scooped me up in his big powerful arms and tried to quiet me.

When my tears finally subsided, I told him the entire story – how this man had been raping me for months and that I thought I'd killed him. My father immediately went into crisis-control mode. He washed me up, threw away my bloody clothes, and asked if anyone had seen me or witnessed the incident. I told him that I didn't think so. He gave both of us ice cream like he always did for me after having sex.

We watched the news, waiting to hear about the stabbing in the alley at 68th and Main Street. In this case, no news was good news. As usual, what happens in the hood, stays in the hood. Nobody cares about the poor Blacks and Latinos on the Eastside.

You could say that I got away with murder, but no ill-deed goes unpaid. I was not only a murderer I was very mean to my father in his last years. But I was a good sister. I took great care of the house, my brothers who were seldom there, and my baby sister. When our father finally died, my siblings were used to me taking care of them and our lives didn't change that much.

• • • • •

CH 17 – CARLA
Having My Babies

My guilt, pain and anger fueled my need for more and more alcohol. I weighed a little more than a 100 pounds but could drink a gallon of alcohol a day. If I had been into opioids that much, I would be dead by now. I would drink sometimes until I blacked out. But most times before that happened, I'd find someone to curse out and fight.

I'm now 36. I have five children with five different fathers. They were all younger than me. I guess I needed to be the oldest because older was power. Plus, the younger men I chose were all slender built, so if we ever got into fights, I could hold my own. My days of being overpowered were over.

I had my first child at eighteen. When I discovered I was pregnant, I stopped drinking cold turkey. I was looking forward to having something I could call my own. I was able to get Section 8 Housing and had to pay only $79 monthly.

Jermaine came here screaming loud and healthy. He weighed 6 lbs., 4 oz. He was the most beautiful baby I'd ever seen. I know, every mother thinks that, but my baby truly was. His caramel-colored face was framed with dark brown curls. He had big beautiful light-brown eyes and eyelashes that many models would die for. His father was sixteen. At eighteen, he just had his first child – a little baby girl. I'm a grandmother at thirty-six.

My second child was a beautiful little girl, weighing 5 lbs., 12 oz. Her father was seventeen. When his mother found out that her son had fathered a child with an older lady, she threatened to have me arrested. I had to hide out at my Grannie's until I was able to find another place to live in order to escape her wrath.

That girl grew up to be my brightest child. She was admitted to a special school for gifted children and earned straight A's. Not only was she smart, but she was beautiful. She was very developed by the age of twelve. She couldn't walk down the street without men honking and hollering at her. She had attitude. I liked that to an extent. I didn't like it when she acted like she was better than everyone else. She has dreams and goals and I'm sure she'll reach them. She's a fighter like her mother.

My third and fourth child were twin boys. They were so tiny — one was 3 lbs., 11 oz.; the other was 4 lbs., 3 oz. It was three weeks before they had gained enough weight to come home with me. I had started back drinking – not as much as before – but drinking while pregnant is a no-no I know. I prayed that the doctor wouldn't discover my dirty little secret and take my kids away. That has always been my biggest fear. I live daily with the knowledge that both boys have learning disabilities because of my actions.

My last child was also a boy. I named him Drake – one of my favorite singers. He was my largest baby, weighing in at a whopping 7 lb., 4 oz.! He had the sweetest temperament of all my babies. He was smart and full of personality. When he became school-age, he was always the teacher's pet. During that pregnancy I had cleaned up my act and stopped drinking – perhaps that's why he was so different from the middle three.

Drake was a little baby, about eight months, when Dr. Jefferson introduced me to Ms. Sweet. I remembered seeing her around campus years ago. She still looked the same. I nervously answered the questions she fired at me and was told that she'd call me after she made her decision.

I didn't have long to wait because she called me that evening around five o'clock. She told me that, even though I hadn't gotten my high school diploma, she'd hire me as an art teacher. I would oversee three classes for four days and I'd be paid under the table out of her pocket. I was so excited, but nervous at the same time.

Ch. 18 - CARLA
Redemption

Because of that position, my self-esteem soared. I was now being referred to as Ms. Stone. Ms. Sweet helped me develop lesson plans, helped me with my presentations, taught me the grading procedures, roll taking – everything. I, of course, didn't curse at school but I did cut down on my cursing at home. I developed more patience and tolerance with my kids. I enrolled in a continuation school and after two semesters, received my diploma.

I was still teaching at the YouthBuild school when I graduated and so I was asked to chaperone the prom. I'd always regretted not graduating and experiencing all of the activities that seniors have. Not only did I go to the prom, but also grad night at Magic Mountain and the senior picnic.

Ms. Sweet encouraged me to forgive my mom and to reach out to her in prison, which I did. She also had me journaling and writing a book about my life. I never finished the book, but I gained a lot of insight and peace while I was writing. Helping my kids with their homework, preparing meals and lunches, taking care of the household – just being a single mother is taxing.

• • • • •

Last year all of my work and sacrifices paid off. Between me and all my children, we received 25 certificates! Some for perfect attendance, some for most improved, me for attending all PTA meetings and conferences and most supportive parent – just to name a few. If I sound like a proud parent, I am. I am that and more.

I am extremely blessed and highly favored. My pastor and his wife have been just as supportive as Ms. Sweet and Dr. Jefferson. Even when I've had to kick ass or curse someone out at church, they never kicked me out. They could counsel me, reprimand me and continue their love and support. My children flourished under their leadership, as well.

Recently, I was voted president of the PTA at my kids' school and offered a position as a Special Education Teacher's Aide, as well. My family and friends are as happy as I am about my successes. Not only that, I've just completed my first semester at L.A. Trade-Technical College. I plan to get my A.A. degree and then transfer to USC to get my BA in Psychology.

My children and I go to church every Sunday. I teach the teen-age Sunday School class, which I love. I enjoy preparing and delivering lessons – thanks to Ms. Sweet. My daughter is the lead dancer in the praise dance team and my sons enjoy all of the many church activities. On Saturdays, they help me prepare meals such as spaghetti and chili beans and rice to feed the homeless in our area.

I love that my children have the gift of giving, like me. I have come a long way from the fighting fool that I was. Today, I'm at peace with myself. I have asked God for forgiveness of the murder, my father's mal-treatment and all of the people who I've cursed out and beat up. More than that, I have forgiven myself. I am a good employee, a good student, a loving, giving person and a great mother. I'm real proud of me. I've found redemption for all the bad and I'm so glad.

• • • • •

CH. 19 – CIW
California Institution for Women

Carla has made me so very proud of her and her achievements. She could have easily been one of the women that I met at CIW. I hadn't heard anything about the California Institution for Women, let alone, knew what it was. I had been to quite a few men's prisons visiting brothers, friends, and wayward students. I'd never been to a women's prison because I'd never known any female who went to prison. I couldn't believe that I could just drive onto the facility's parking lot without having my trunk checked by the armed guards at the front gate.

I found a parking space in the already crowded unpaved parking lot. After walking about a block in my two-inch heels (I'd been forewarned about wearing comfortable shoes) to the check-in window, I was met by Rebecca Weicker, the founder of Justice Reform and about fifteen other members of the symposium.

After following the visitation formalities which included having our driver's licenses checked and returned, twenty minutes later we were ushered into a cavernous room which I figured was a gymnasium only because of the basketball hoops at each end. There were no bleachers.

We were instructed to arrive at 8:00 in the morning for check-in and the symposium was scheduled to kick off at 9:00. It was only 8:30 but people were already seated in their specified group noted on their name tags. I found mine and slapped it on my chest and quickly made my way over to the table set up with donuts, muffins, bagels, coffee cake, Starbucks coffee and orange juice.

As I made my way to my circle for the day, I hugged and kissed four ladies that I knew. Minutes later, I was seated with my group munching on my muffin and drinking my three-sugared coffee with lots of milk (I'm not a coffee drinker. I used to say 'cause coffee is for grown-ups). Everyone was there but one, Noelle, and she arrived only minutes after me. There was a DA and a representative from Victims of Crime and a lady from the mayor's office and the four murderers. They looked just like us except for their light blue prison garb.

There were two Caucasians, one Latino and one Black. I have to say that I was happy to see such a small number of African-American inmates.

One of the issues highlighted by the Women's March on Washington was the mass incarceration of women. Although the U.S. imprisonment rate has been declining for almost a decade, the size of the female inmate population is being maintained by surging imprisonment of whom? White women. Over the past fifteen years, Black women prison population has decreased to half while the number of white women incarcerated has increased.

We started off with us, the victims, sharing our stories. They shed tears of sympathy for us, the survivors. I could see that this was going to be a successful symposium for healing and forgiveness.

•　　•　　•　　•　　•

CH. 20 – RITA
My Childhood

I have to admit that Rita was one of my favorites. She was about 5'4", an inch shorter than me. Her hair was shoulder length and curled. Her make-up was impeccable. She was a lovely, curvaceous Latina. Her ACE score was 8. (Please refer to ACE Survey). Prior to her 18th birthday, she had experienced all of them except #3 and #5). This is her story:

• • • • •

On November 22, 1964, I was born and then put up for adoption. A foster parent raised me until I was one year old, then I was adopted. My father was an ex-gang member, a high school drop-out, and had the visible scars from stab wounds on his back. He also served in the U.S. Army with an honorable discharge. His parents were alcoholics and both died in a car accident. I never had the chance to meet my grandparents.

My father was also an alcoholic who had taken over the responsibility of raising all 14 of his siblings. My mother was a schoolgirl who never got into trouble and graduated from high school. Her parents were involved in her life and she was "Daddy's little girl". She was the youngest of five girls. My mother was very co-dependent.

•　　•　　•　　•　　•

At nine years old, I was told about my adoption status. All of my siblings were adopted and were not biologically related, with the exception of my twin sister and I. We were adopted together. My parents wanted us to know before we were told by anyone else.

As I was growing up, I was always the target of my father's drunken rages. He would look for me, and then my mother. The arguments were always about my father's late-night mysterious locations. I would protect my mother simply by keeping an eye on her as I knew when he came home, the arguing would ensue. His displaced anger went as far as him pointing a gun at my mother's head.

Things worsened over time. My mother woke me up in the middle of the night to spy on my father. We would stake out his whereabouts. My mother would awaken me from sleeping in the back seat and we would spy on my father as we followed him in her car. She wanted to see if he was with another woman.

We discovered that he indeed was cheating and was involved with running drugs and guns. He was deeply involved with illegal drug activities. His activities continued well into my teen-age years. Meanwhile, I was still being physically abused by my enraged father and I'd always escape to the neighbor's house.

Eventually, I ran away for good. I'd like to add that my father was a good provider because we had everything like clothes, cars, food, a nice home and we went on lots of vacations. My father usually stayed behind, which allowed him to continue with his illegal activities.

I loved going to school just to escape my dysfunctional home life. I played every sport offered, but I really loved swimming. I made it on the swim team in high school. Things changed in my teen-age years; I started drinking at age fifteen and became involved with someone I really liked. I lost my virginity to him and we stayed together, on and off, for about two years. I also enjoyed photography and I graduated in 1982.

After graduation, I experimented with cocaine at a beach party. I didn't get addicted to that drug for the simple fact that I hated that numb feeling. I continued to drink. I met a guy named Alex who I believed really loved me. Boy, was that a mistake! This guy replaced my father's physical abuse in my life and he was ten times worse!

I became his robot, doing exactly what he ordered me to do. He cheated on me and was an alcoholic and an addict. I experienced meth use while involved with him. Eventually, I was beaten so badly when I was five months pregnant that I was hospitalized and later tried to leave him. That didn't stop him from hunting me down. Yes, I was terrified that he would kill me.

•　　•　　•　　•　　•

CH. 21 – Rita
My Addictions

When I was twenty-three years old, I started becoming heavy in my addiction, buying my own bag of meth. This led me to selling. This became the dark part of my life, associating with people who were involved with dealing in illegal drugs. I already had the knowledge of how to stalk someone. I learned that from my mother. My life drastically changed at this time – I had the power and control, as well as the drugs and money. I feared nothing and no one anymore.

I began stalking my boyfriends, just like my mother. I would physically fight when I had to. I drank, I used drugs when needed, but making money was more important to me, like it was for my father. I would do hales (jobs) and it didn't matter if and how I left you – dead or alive. If you owed me, you paid — one way or another.

At this time, I decided to ask my mother to take my kids. I was getting involved more and more in the drug world and I could no longer endanger them. One rule I always had and that was not to harm children. If you hurt me in my relationships, I would hurt you back. I didn't know how to exactly, but I did what I had to do to get the attention of those who hurt me, no matter what the cost. I became just like my mother and father.

I was arrested for the first time at the age of 27 for two counts of assault with a deadly weapon. The weapon in this case was my vehicle. I bailed out of jail, but also received another case of battery, in which I took a deal of 60 days. After that, I had two more battery charges. Then, vandalism, fraud, manufacturing and burglary. I was released on my own recognizance after doing 101 days. I always fought to stay out of prison, so I ended up doing county time for those charges. My last charge of burglary was a deal that I took from 6 years to 2 years, down to 1 year in the County Jail. I completed the one year in the County.

It was there where I met my victim, Donald Peterson, in this co-ed county jail. I had only 4 and a half months to go. I was working in the Administrative Office, cleaning; attending computer school in the afternoon; and working in the laundry at night. I would hear the girls talking about him. I had to check out who they were talking about. Long blonde hair, blue eyes, 6'3", 225 lbs. "Not bad", I thought.

I started getting kites from him and seeing him throughout the jail. (In a jail or prison, the term kite refers to a written request for something). We flirted, even though I had a female correctional officer warn me that he was no good. Of course, I didn't listen because I was going to get what I wanted and I wanted him.

I thought I was going to be released before him, but a lieutenant and CO informed me that I wasn't being released, but transferred to Riverside County Jail and then to the West Valley Detention Center. I had a warrant for not completing my weekends for previous charges. Don and I were able to see each other before I was transferred. He stayed in contact with me while I served the remainder of my time in the other counties and he wanted to hook up with me when we got of jail.

We did, and he made me agree not to bring any drugs or alcohol to his brother's house where he was residing. I agreed to an extent. After getting out of jail, I could drink without getting in trouble with my probation officer. I loved drinking and so I drank despite his wishes. I went to his brother's house and we finally physically touched. And you know the rest.

I became more deeply involved with Don, but then my ex-boyfriend prior to my jail terms tried to pop back into my life. He had his nerve because he hadn't contacted me during my county time. I no longer wanted anything to do with him. He knew I was involved with Don but he didn't care. He was going to have me too.

I said, "The hell you are!" and we physically fought. We fought so badly that he had to go to the hospital because he was bleeding so badly. I didn't care. When Don saw my face, he asked what happened and I told him. At that point, he wanted to fight my ex., but I didn't let it happen.

• • • • •

CH. 22 – RITA
Lies & Insecurities

I needed money so I started selling drugs again. I thought, "Why not? I can keep this from Don". I needed to regain my home, a car – everything I'd lost while being incarcerated. I had a secret life – again following in my father's footsteps. Don wanted us to live together but I explained that it would be best if we got our own place. I didn't want to live with anybody. I never wanted to share my space with anyone else. I'd always had my own place. In the meantime, Don convinced me to move into his brother Kenny's two-story home. We were all getting along just fine. I started calling Kenny my big brother.

After I moved in, Don became really possessive. He'd page me over and over, contacting my twin sister to find out my location and why I wasn't answering his pages. I'd returned to the drug world and met a new business partner, Miko. I told Don I was looking for a job when, in fact, I was out doing business. I had so many secrets that Don never knew about. My attitude was drifting further and further away from him. Remember, no one could gain control of me.

One day I was drinking, did some meth and was Spring cleaning while enjoying my loud music. I made dinner and everything was going great until I found letters addressed to Don from women in jail. He was going to go fishing with one, sent another one money, another one wrote introducing herself, and the last one was a woman that I'd done time with.

I contacted her. She was married and didn't want anything to do with Don. She claimed she wanted her marriage to work and Don was the one contacting her. I wrote the other girls to inform them about us and since they already knew where we lived, they could come see me if they insisted on continuing to contact him. Meaning I would fight them if they tried.

•   •   •   •   •

CH 23 - RITA
The Day Before

I was dropped off from "looking for a job" – that's what I told Don. He had been looking for me, interrogating me. He asked where I was, who I was with, and why. He irritated me with his questioning. Upset that I had read his mail, he threw me to the ground when I told him about the jail letters I had found. I had been holding a grudge against him for that for a while. That was the first red flag. I finally told him I was leaving. I didn't want to stay there anymore. I gave the keys back to Kenny and told him also that I was leaving.

I was looking for a ride away from there. While awaiting my ride, I went into the garage and started drinking. I realized that I had left my purse inside our bedroom, so I started tapping the ceiling of the garage with the broom handle to gain Don's attention to come downstairs. What I really wanted was for us to talk. I wanted to feel that he still wanted me and didn't want me to go. This was a learned behavior I witnessed from my mother and father – the physical fighting, followed by making up.

I sat there waiting for Miko to return my call when I saw a knife and started to sharpen it. There was no reason for me to pick it up other than I was killing time. I loved knives. I decided to go upstairs to knock on the door to ask for my purse since Don hadn't budged. I thought we could mend our broken relationship, but instead we had words.

Don came out and dragged me down the stairs and slammed my head into the door with great force. His brother heard everything and did nothing. He just walked back into his room as if this was just a normal thing.

I finally got ahold of Miko, telling him to meet me at the nearby gas station. I went to Kenny and begged him to give me a ride to the gas station. He agreed. I let him know that I would be back the next day to get my belongings, asking when would be the best time when Don wasn't home. We arranged for 6:00 the next morning. Miko dropped me off at Yard Dogs. This was a hangout place.

•　　•　　•　　•　　•

CH. 24 – RITA
Wildin' Out

Isaw my ex there at Yard Dogs. He was so high. He had borrowed his brother's car and I asked him if I could use it and he agreed, but told me to be back by a certain time because his brother needed to go to work.

I saw this runaway girl there. Her name was Adina. I asked if she would come with me to pick up my belongings and she agreed. I had met Adina before when she needed to shower and change her clothes.

I went to Benny's house first to let him know what had happened. Miko and Benny were friends. Benny was the one who introduced me to Miko. Benny did the running for us, if needed. I was ready to leave – to go back to Kenny's house to get my things.

I could have made the decision to cut my losses and not return to Kenny's but I didn't. I went against my gut instincts. Benny stopped me at the door, handing me a knife clothed in a sheath and said, "Here, if that puto puts his hands on you, you know what to do".

At that time, I should have said, "No, I don't need the knife, I just want to get my stuff." But instead, I took the knife, knowing that I would use it. I went back to the car and took off, on my way to get my stuff.

As we're driving on the freeway, I'm coaching Adina to keep an eye on everything and if Don puts his hands on me and she sees it, to tell the cops everything that she saw. My needs were the only thing that concerned me at the moment. I didn't want to go back to jail. I could give a hoot what happened to Adina.

While driving, I noticed Adina staring at my face. "What?" I asked. She didn't reply. I then looked in the mirror and saw the bruising on my face that she'd been staring at. It was the result of Don throwing me against the front door. That was an instant trigger. I became enraged. My thought process was, he's going to pay for this.

•   •   •   •   •

I parked the car and put the knife at the side of my hip inside my sweatpants and said to Adina, "Let's go!" we proceeded to walk up to the front door. I saw that the door was opened; only the screen was shut. I could see Don in the kitchen, smoking. This was yet another opportunity for me to just turn around, but I didn't. Kenny came to the door and gave me permission to go get my belongings. Adina went with me upstairs. We got some of my things and took them to the car. We returned to the house where Don was still seated at the table, still smoking.

Adina went upstairs, but I decided to tell this SOB about what he did to my face. I went into the kitchen and he immediately got up and told me to get out and get away from him. He yelled for his brother to put me out of their house, but I was determined to tell him off. I pointed to my face, saying, "Look, you SOB, look what you did! I'm gonna have my homeboys take care of you!" He didn't care about anything I was saying. He ignored me. I wanted his attention, but I wasn't getting it.

We heard a honk from a vehicle outside and Don proceeded to get his things. It was his boss picking him up for work. I followed him out the front door, even though I feared abandonment. All I wanted was to be loved and accepted by him. I wished things were different. Mainly, I didn't want to be alone.

●　　　●　　　●　　　●　　　●

He had his lunch box and his cup of coffee. He started throwing the coffee directly at my face, yelling, "Bitch, get away from me!!" Adina was right behind me. I kept walking behind him, allowing the thrown hot coffee to splatter on my face. I saw his boss sitting in his truck. Don and I were now in the middle of the street and I kept running my mouth. Don turned around and socked me. We started physically fighting then.

All I remembered was falling down to the ground, my face was that close to the pavement. I flashbacked to my father teaching me not to let anyone take me down. This was an indication of weakness. I wasn't that strong; this was a learned behavior that I lived by my whole life. He continued to hit me. His boss stayed in the truck, observing the entire event. Not once stepping out to help me.

Don ran to the passenger side truck door and open it. I followed right behind him. I was filled with so much rage. I kept running my mouth while my knife remained concealed in my pants. I then ran to my car and he was right behind me. I turned around and we were face to face. I grabbed my knife with my left hand and stabbed him. His blood gushed all over me like a water hose. He ran back to his boss's truck, shouting, "That bitch just stabbed me!!"

I saw Adina standing on the curb and shouted to her that we needed to leave. I could have run to help Don; I could have called 911. But instead, I ran like I had always done when my father beat me. I knew in that moment that I was going back to jail. I still had the bloody knife in my grasp. I started to hand Adina the knife but changed my mind and decided to hold onto it as I drove off.

I knew not to take the freeway because I knew the cops would be waiting for me on the offramp. I used the back roads. I thought about throwing the knife out the window, but didn't. I dropped off Adina at Yard Dogs. I was covered in blood and she was terrified, exclaiming, "You need to take a shower and get all that blood off you."

•   •   •   •   •

I went to Benny's, but he was not home. Two other females were. I knew one of them through Miko. I explained that I needed to take a shower. I asked if they could help me wash the car to remove all the blood from it. They agreed. Showering, I watched Don's blood cascading down my body, rinsing down the drain. After showering, to wash the blood off the knife, I used the kitchen sink.

Benny returned home and I told him what happened. I told him that I had possibly stabbed Don in the heart. He was still alive when I last saw him running and yelling. I assumed that I would go to jail for attempted manslaughter or for one count of assault with a deadly weapon. Either way, I knew I was going to jail. I felt for certain I was going to be caught.

I placed the evidence – my bloody clothes, the knife, my boots with the splattered blood in a plastic shopping bag and handed it to Benny to discard. I had him bury the evidence like I'd seen on TV. I never knew where and will never know because Benny was killed in an automobile accident months later.

After the chaos I endured that day, I wanted to escape. I needed to get high. It had not occurred to me to worry about what happened to Don. Was he in the hospital? I did not care at that point. I was hurt and heartbroken. I just wanted to get dope so I could relieve my pain. Benny and I drove to look for Miko. Unfortunately, he was not at home. As we went searching for Alfonso, I saw the Corona PD. To me, they appeared to be looking for something or someone. I was angry that he had already called the police.

We went by my mother's house. Her driveway gate was open, so we drove right in. I yelled for my brother to shut it before the cops could see me. I let Benny know that no way I was going to drive around. I dropped him off at his house, then went to Yard Dogs to get Richard, my ex, so I could return Sammy's car. Sammy was Richard's brother. Richard was so out of it because he was stupid high. I drove to his brother's apartment with Richard in the passenger seat. I drove by the parking lot and noticed a car full of undercover cops.

"That muthafucker called the police!" I exclaimed as I drove past the parking lot where they were. I parked the car and ran up to the apartment while Richard stayed in the car. I went into the apartment and peered outside to see what was going on outside. I was unsure what it was, but I had an eerie feeling that I wasn't getting away this time. I was caught!

I did not understand why it took so long for the undercover cops to knock on the apartment door. I later learned that they had to wait for a search warrant to proceed. I put the car keys on the tracking of the closet door, then I hid in one of the hallway cabinets.

They busted into the apartment looking for me. They found me when they searched and opened the cabinet door. All of them had guns drawn, pointed directly at me. One Latino officer even held his gun point blank range to my head. They handcuffed, searched me and escorted me outside.

Sitting on the curb, I wondered, "Why are all these cops here?" They placed me in the rear seat of the police car. When they jumped on the freeway, I was really confused. I couldn't fathom why they took the freeway instead of the streets to the police department. They got off at an offramp and drove behind a restaurant where I was transferred to a different undercover car.

I had talked with the officer while I waited in the car, trying to gauge exactly what was really happening. He was tight-lipped, but mentioned something about 25 years to life. At that moment, I realized this was much more serious than I initially thought.

•   •   •   •   •

CH 25 - RITA
D-Day

I was now being interrogated where I admitted to the stabbing. I still had the defensive injuries showing why I had stabbed him. I finally accepted the fact that I would do time for attempted murder, manslaughter, assault with a deadly weapon, and/or whatever else they wanted to charge me with. I just wanted to put this behind me. They wanted to know the location of the knife. I lied and told them that I'd thrown it out the window after fleeing the crime scene. They asked for its location and I fabricated its location. The homicide task force detectives searched for it in the rain and came back empty-handed.

They further interrogated me so much that I requested a call to my lawyer. They denied it, even though I had articulated that I had rights too. They finally revealed to me that Don was dead. DEAD?! What? I collapsed, crying. I had NO IDEA!

I was transported to the hospital for my injuries and then booked into the county jail for first degree murder. I later found out that Don made it to the driveway, where his brother applied pressure to his neck, trying to stop the bleeding. When he arrived at the hospital, he was DOA. Don had bled to death 60 minutes after I stabbed him, severing his jugular vein. The force of the stabbing, chipped his collar bone and the knife almost went through his back.

After fighting my case in the county, I was finally sentenced to second degree murder, a crime that carried 15 years to life. Plus, an enhancement of 21 to life for being a second striker, for a grand total of 36 years to life.

I have been imprisoned for 20 years now and I regret my decisions every day of my life. I sought redemption by writing the following letter to Don even though he'll never read it. I hope he's smiling down and forgiving me.

•   •   •   •   •

CH 26 - RITA
Redemption

Dear Don;

I know I have taken so much from your family and friends. I know that every day of my life I have to live with the fact that I cannot change what I've done. I callously stabbed you, severing your jugular vein as you laid there bleeding to death in the drive-way, I ran from the scene with no remorse. Not only did I not help you, I did not call 911.

I later learned that I had killed you before we arrived at the Kaiser Hospital. I think of your mother, father, and siblings, and your three boys hearing about your death and how I had murdered you. I think of the holidays, birthdays, graduations, weddings, the birth of your grandchildren, and so much, much more. I can honestly say that I think mostly of the pain that I've caused your family. I also realize that my actions affected the entire community.

I was that monster they labeled me in court and a very callous woman. I didn't care what I'd done – it was all about me and my insecurities. I see who I was and I see who I am today. I know I deserve to be in prison for your death and the pain I've caused your family and friends. I wholeheartedly accept that. If there is anything I would say to you, it would be, "I am deeply sorry for taking your life and with your death I have been able to recognize my actions in depths of my insecurities, my addiction and my violent behaviors. Today, I want to honor your death. I want to tell your family and children, the truth of what happened that day I killed you. They deserve to know the truth".

I will never forget what your father said on the stand. His words still remain stuck in my head – "We can't forgive Rita right now". I hold onto those words, but fervently hope that one day they will.

Because of your death, I am the person that I am today. I never again want to be the person I was. I make positive choices; I stay in my recovery; I work on my self-esteem; my self-worth. Most of all, I want to be honest. Don, I am truly, truly sorry.

Rita

CH 27 – KIERRA
My Childhood

Kierra was another woman in our group at CIW. She had an ACE score of 8. The two ACEs that she didn't experience were #3 and #10. She was a tall, chocolate-colored woman. Her hair was beautifully corn-rolled. She made that light blue jumpsuit look hot. She was wearing the latest Jordan's. I later found out that they were supplied by her wife. I found out that if you had people on the outside with money, you could get whatever you wanted. Here's Kierra's story about her journey to CIW.

●　　●　　●　　●　　●

I am the oldest of eleven children. Amongst all of us, we had eight fathers. Simply put: my mother fucked a lot of men — without protection. It's a wonder why she never got AIDS. I'm sure she contracted all of the other venereal diseases.

Needless to say, my mother was crack addicted and an alcoholic. So, you know where that left me, the responsible one, the one to take care of the siblings. Caring for my siblings meant cooking, cleaning, doing the laundry, getting them ready for school, helping with homework and everything else.

I missed a lot of school days because I was tired. After the kids went off to school and daycare, I'd take the time to relax, watching TV and reading. I was an avid reader. I could escape into another world through books. I'd be transported to another city – hell, another country. I could be a princess, an only child - rich and beautiful. Books took me away from the everyday drudgery of raising kids and a trifling-ass mother.

I just had my nineteenth birthday when I got home and found my mother face down on her bedroom floor. I felt her body. It was cold. I felt for a pulse. There was none. Panicked, I dialed 911. "I think my mom is dead!" I screamed into the phone.

It took almost a half hour before the paramedics arrived. I was a total wreck. I was glad my siblings were at school. I texted my girlfriend, Treasure, who was now attending Los Angeles Trade Technical College.

I had no interest in men. I hadn't seen any positive manly images in my neighborhood. My mother's suitors certainly weren't worth a damn. We were on welfare because none of her babies' fathers paid child support. I'm not sure, and neither was she, of the real identities of a couple of my siblings' fathers.

I was never molested or raped. That's not my story for the reason I'm gay. I guess I was born that way. Even though I grew up doing womanly duties like cooking and cleaning, I was a tomboy. I liked wearing pants and I kept my hair cut short because I didn't have time to be messing with it. I certainly didn't have the time or money to be buying wigs and fake-ass hair.

●　　●　　●　　●　　●

CH 28 – KIERRA
My Treasure

Yeah, I was gay because I liked girls – nothing biological. Growing up, I was a tomboy. I didn't like doing girly things, but I liked being around the girls. I liked this one girl in particular. She was in my fifth-grade class. She was quiet and shy and sat in the last row in the back of the classroom.

She was caramel-colored with a headful of long wild curls cascading down her back. She was obviously bi-racial. I would day-dream about kissing her whenever I needed to escape the real days' challenges.

I got to know her better at recess. I was in line behind her waiting my turn at the tether ball. Although she was a passive little girl, I can tell you that girl became aggressive and competitive when she got up to that tether ball pole.

After beating the boy who won the last round, it was my turn to step to the pole. "Are you ready for your ass whipping?" She surprised me with those challenging words. And she backed it up. She whopped my ass fair and square *and* fast. I had to give her props.

We became BFFs right then and there. We were inseparable at school. She was a good listener – something I sorely needed. I'll always remember the first time we kissed. It was at lunch behind the girls' bathroom. That's when we became more than just best friends.

We had similar backgrounds. She didn't know her father, like me, and her mother was a crackhead, like mine. Only now she was in a foster home because her mom had been incarcerated.

One day she came to school with a huge bruise on her upper arm. She had tried to hide it, but I saw it and asked her about it. She was reluctant to talk about it but when I put my arms around her, hugging her to my breasts, she burst into body-wracking sobs. When she finally quieted down, she shared all of the atrocities she suffered at the hands of her caretakers. I vowed silently to myself that I would be there for her – whenever, for whatever and always.

I was heartbroken when she was transferred to another group home clear across town. We couldn't see each other like we used to but we chatted daily on our cell phones. We were finally re-united when she moved in with us after aging out of the system at eighteen.

•   •   •   •   •

CH 29 – KIERRA
D-Day

Just thinking about the prospect of being separated from my siblings was frightening. I had been the one who looked after them and all of their needs. My mother was the one with the EBT card the one who communicated with the social service people. What were we going to do? How would we eat? Rent was only $35 monthly because we had Section 8 housing.

We were able to survive for about two months after our mother's demise. When the lights and gas were turned off, I had to make some serious decisions and moves. The last thing I wanted was to lose my siblings to the system.

I'd aged out and I found out that I could petition to care for my siblings and that way we could continue living in our apartment and still get the same assistance. The application process and visits from DPSS took forever. Eventually, we were totally out of money and resources.

I thought and thought and I, like the young fool I was, came up with this ridiculous idea and decided to act on it. That's the answer! I would rob the neighborhood mini-market. I knew that one of my homies, Jeffrey, had several guns. I called him and was able to borrow one of his guns because of my contrived story about a break-in at our place and we needed protection.

Here's the plan. I had been casing the mini-mart four blocks away. I knew when Mr. Kim would be at the cash register alone. I didn't tell my girl or anyone. I put on my ski mask and gloves and waited until the mart emptied of customers.

I entered the mart and spoke in a low voice, like a man, "Open the register and give me all your money!"

Mr. Kim was shaking, "Please don't shoot," he begged.

"I don't want to shoot you. Just give me the money!" I yelled.

He opened the cash register with one hand and with the other hand, he grabbed his gun. Seeing all this happening at once, I panicked, shot him in his shoulder and ran out the mart, leaving the money behind. Talk about a bungled robbery!

My foolery doesn't end there. I ran home like a fool. I was captured on camera inside and outside the mart.

There were also witnesses who heard the shot and aided the police to track me down.

• • • • •

It didn't take long before we were surrounded by a million police it seemed. A helicopter was hovering above, its lights penetrating the darkness. The forceful knock at the door wasn't quelled at all by its loud engine.

All of my siblings were screaming and hollering. Treasure had this, "What the hell did you do?" look on her face. I quickly opened the door before it came crashing in on all of us. All I could see were the barrels of a thousand guns pointed right at me. I had my hands in the air like at the concerts where we just didn't care.

Right behind them were what I learned later were social workers. What I'd dreaded was happening – thanks to my dumb ass.

• • • • •

I was in the Twin Towers it seemed for months before I finally went to trial. I didn't know that I'd actually murdered Mr. Kim. I'd shot him in the shoulder, for heaven's sake. I prayed that that one shot hadn't been fatal, but my prayers went unanswered. I learned that

Mr. Kim had developed a blood clot that traveled from his shoulder to his heart and that's what killed him. I was flabbergasted.

My public pretender wasn't worth a damn. He was a waste of human skin as far as I was concerned. After all of the evidence was submitted, even though I was young and had a clean record, I was given 30 to life.

I was so overwhelmed with the verdict that I felt my spirit leave my body as I lapsed into unconsciousness. When I came to, I remembered the sentencing and blacked out again. Paramedics were quickly on hand and gave me oxygen. I knew all my family and my girl, Treasure, were in the room, but I couldn't look back at them as I was led away – cuffed, defeated, ashamed and hopeless.

I hated God and his heavenly crew. I hated my court-appointed attorney, I hate the jurors, I hated the judge. I even hated my siblings and Treasure because they were the motivating force behind what I did. But, no doubt, I hated my mother most of all.

•　　•　　•　　•　　•

CH 30 - KIERRA
Accountability

Being locked up like a caged animal gave me plenty of time to think. Seeing Treasure helped me keep my sanity. Just knowing that I'd be getting a visit from her kept me grounded, encouraged and hopeful. She informed me that she was able to keep the house we shared, had a good-paying job and was working on fostering my siblings. That glimmer of hope helped me immensely.

For the first five years, I was consumed with self-pity — blaming everyone and everything for my situation. I was the proverbial angry black woman. I got thrown in the hole for fighting too many times to remember. I couldn't get any visitors while in the hole and the letters that I'd receive from Treasure finally got my dumb-ass to chill out. I learned to control my temper so that I could see her – my rock, my love.

One of my most memorable visits was when Treasure informed me that she had been awarded custody of the remaining siblings. The oldest twins and two other siblings had moved out shortly after my arrest, leaving Treasure to care for the rest.

On June 18, 2008, the court ruled in favor of same-sex marriages in the state of California. On July 4, 2008, we exchanged vows. I surely wasn't going to get into any more altercations after that. With marriage, came conjugal visits. Four times a year, my wife and I could spend an entire weekend together in our own apartment doing whatever we wanted which included watching TV, eating, and lots of good loving.

• • • • •

CH 31 – KIERRA
Redemption

For the past fifteen years, I've been an exemplary inmate. Whatever opportunity, class, or workshop was offered, I took it. I've received certificates in anger management, financial and computer literacy, drug and alcohol counseling. I have an A.A. in liberal arts and a B.A. in Psychology. So, you see, I have been working hard to show myself worthy to be released.

I'm scheduled to go before the parole board later this year. Not only will I be able to show the certificates and my degrees but I have certificates that I received from Ms. Weicker's Justice Reform Symposiums. Meeting Bettye at one of the symposiums was the highlight of these symposiums. Her openness and willingness to bear her soul and feelings made us want to reciprocate the same energy.

I can't say that I've never cried as much as in that meeting because I've cried me a river in my little lifetime, but I can say that we had to request another box of Kleenex. The closeness, love and forgiveness that we received from Bettye and the others was unlike anything I've ever experienced. The closest thing I could compare it with was the feeling I received when I was twelve and baptized.

Another thing we got from the symposiums was the ability to look deep within ourselves and be remorseful over the pain and damage that we caused. Part of the healing process for both parties was forgiveness. We were asked to write a letter to our victim's family and I agreed. Treasure had gotten Mr. Kim's son's name and address for me. Mr. Kim had lost his wife to cancer years earlier. I didn't know how difficult that task would be. Finally, after about twenty rewrites, here it is:

•   •   •   •   •

Dear Jung Kim:

I hope that you don't mind that my wife got me your name and address but I so wanted to contact you and let you know how deeply sorry I am for murdering your father. I regret what I did each and every day of my life! There's not a day goes by that

I don't think about that horrible day that changed so many lives. I will live with that knowledge for the rest of my life.

You deserve to know what happened. My mother had overdosed and left me to care for my nine siblings. We were out of money and resources (I know that's no excuse to take a life) so I thought that Mr. Kim would hand over the money without a fight, but I was wrong.

I murdered a good man – a great father and businessman and for this, I am so, so sorry. I am asking, no – begging your forgiveness. I'll understand if you can't but if you can find it in your heart to forgive me, I'd be more than grateful. Hoping to hear from you.

Kierra Holman

•   •   •   •   •

I was grateful that Bettye was interested enough in my story to be asked to share it, along with the other women in her book. Wow, never thought I'd be in a book.

Hopefully, I can exit these prison gates in 2021. All of my siblings will be grown and on their own. Treasure and I will have the place all to ourselves. With my certificates and degrees, I should have no problem finding employment. I'll only be 42. Two of my sisters and three of my brothers have children. I guess that makes me an aunt/grandmother.

My journey has been a life of ups and downs, curves, detours, potholes, and ditches, but I, too, am the thriver that Bettye Sweet speaks about.

•　　•　　•　　•　　•

CH 32 - DANIELLE
White Girl in Here?

Kierra and Carla were both African-Americans and Rita was Latina. That's why when I visited CIW for the Justice Reform Symposium, I was surprised to see that only 25% of the inmates were African-Americans. The rest were comprised of whites and Hispanics.

Later, after researching, I learned Keith Humphreys, a Professor of Psychiatry at Stanford University, wrote an article in the *Washington Post* (January 24, 2017) about the rise in the number of white women being incarcerated. He stated that Black women remain imprisoned at a higher rate than white women, but the gap has shrunk from about 7 to 1 in 1985 to about 2 to 1 in 2015. Because whites are a much larger population, the increase in white female imprisonment has easily refilled the prison cells that Black women have been vacating.

At the end of 2015, white women (52,700) outnumbered Black women (21,700) in prison by 2.5 to 1.

But why? Every family has problems and issues. What makes one family dysfunctional and the other functional is how they deal with the problems and/or issues. Problems with alcohol are up among white women but down among Black women. This problem is closely linked to arrests, violence and incarceration.

White women have also been disproportionately affected by the methamphetamine and prescription opioid epidemics – both of which leads to unsavory acts such as stealing, robbing, prostitution and other law-defying activities. Although this is a positive trend for the black women and a negative one for the whites, given present trends that racial gap may soon disappear. If that gap is closed due to continued growth of white female imprisonment, then the total number of women behind bars will dramatically expand rather than shrink.

•　　•　　•　　•　　•

Danielle was one of them - a shy, quiet, soft-spoken, beautiful blue-eyed blonde, standing about 5'5", weighing about 125 lbs. You could see she had a nice figure under that light-blue prison jumpsuit. Her make-up-less face belied her 36 years. Her lovely, silky tresses were tied back, arrested in a long pony tail. Her ACE score was 4 (#3, 4, 8, 9).

The first day of the 2-day symposium at CIW when I met Danielle, her chair was placed about a half foot outside the circle because she was so shy. We all went around the circle sharing our stories – victims and murderers together. Danielle was the third woman to share hers.

We all had to lean in closer in order to hear her. She had been convicted of murder at the tender age of 22. It's true that you can't judge a book by its cover in Danielle's case. She looked like she wouldn't hurt a fly. If you're guessing that she murdered in self-defense, killed an abusive husband or boyfriend, accidently shot a family member or friend, you'd be wrong. I'm not going to tell you who she murdered. I'll let her tell you.

●   ●   ●   ●   ●

CH 33 – DANIELLE
My Parents

My mother, Dominque was born and raised in the picturesque village of Equisheim on the Alsatian Wine Route in France. She was the only child born to Pierre and Bella Lafontaine. Her father – my grandfather – worked in the vineyards and my grandmother was a seamstress. Fashion designing was probably in mother's DNA.

Although Mother grew up poor, she wasn't aware of it because the family always had a place to stay, food to eat, and clean clothes and shoes. She played with the other kids in the village and went to school – just like everyone else.

Dominque's life changed when her parents (my grandparents) were killed in a car accident just two days before her graduation from high school. Mother was now an orphan. She sold all of the family possessions and used that and the meager fortune that my grand-parents had left behind to buy a ticket to Los Angeles, California to start a new life.

She was fortunate enough to find a job as a seam-stress, like my grandmother. She found a rooming house downtown where she rented a room and a shared bath-room. She put all of her energy into her work. She even-tually started making patterns and creating her own designs. In no time at all, she was managing this up and coming top clothing factory.

When she was twenty-five, the owners offered her a part-nership with the company. They had acquired enough money to open a store on Rodeo Drive in Beverly Hills, one of the hottest, most prestigious shopping spots in America. That's when the money really started rolling in. Their clients included such celebrities as Madonna, Betty White, Janet Jackson, Whoopie Goldberg, just to name a few.

The hole and emptiness in Dominique's heart was fi-nally filled when she met Chase Donovan, a dashing, young American pilot. She was on her way to Paris for their annual Spring fashion show when she literally bumped into him in one of the airport coffee shops.

Because of both their demanding work schedules, they were not afforded the time they really wanted to date and get to know one another. It would be ten years later before they finally tied the knot.

CH 34 – DANIELLE
My Childhood

I was born and raised in Bel Air, California, a very desirable neighborhood in the U.S. My brother and I were the only children born to Dominique Lafontaine, a beautiful, successful French fashion designer and handsome airline pilot, Chase Donovan. Mother was in her forties when she had my brother and two years later, she had me.

Most little girls grow up, looking forward to marriage and motherhood. That was not the case with my mother. She didn't marry my father until she was thirty-eight, almost forty. Her career had always consumed her life and she was not ready for the hum -drum life of wife and motherhood.

Father was tall, about 6'2", nicely-built, a manly man. Whenever he was home, you'd find him parked on the couch, watching sports and the news. He would watch

Dr. Phil sometimes, interjecting his views and opinions as if the guests and Dr. Phil could hear him.

It took Father five years before he could get my mother off her birth control pills and agree to have a baby. It was not totally about appeasing her husband, though. She was aware that her time clock was ticking and she wanted to have that experience – but just once.

I was told repeatedly about how long and how much she suffered birthing my brother. She was convinced that she had done her wifely duty by giving her husband a son and determined that there would be no more.

Imagine her chagrin when she discovered that she was pregnant again! Jordan had just had his first birthday. She had taken the home pregnancy test and thrown it in the bathroom trash. She decided she would get an abortion but luckily, Father found the positive pregnancy test results and confronted her. I was told that they had a big argument but he won and eight months later, they had a beautiful baby girl.

My parents didn't have much of a loving relationship. Although I never heard them arguing, I never saw them cuddling, hugging or kissing either. I have no idea what they did behind closed doors. Besides us, what they did in the bedroom could have been the glue that held them together.

Our home was like a mini-castle. I grew up in a house with six bedrooms, seven bathrooms, a jacuzzi, swimming pool, and a tennis court. One would think that would be idyllic but with Father always flying off somewhere, Mother with her business and her social commitments, and my brother, Jordan, doing whatever, I was miserably alone.

Jordan loved playing soccer and watching sports with our father. Sometimes, he would actually find time to play soccer with him in our spacious backyard. Other times, on rare occasions, we would take turns hitting the ball on our tennis court. On even rarer occasions, Mother would join us.

Father and I had a special relationship. His nickname for me was princess D. I missed him terribly when he was away but even as a tiny kid, I knew he had to work. I looked forward to his return home but what I looked forward to even more were the times when Jordan and I would fly with him - right up front in the cockpit!

Mother wasn't very demonstrative, plus I think she was jealous of me and father's relationship. I cannot ever remember her hugging and kissing me. I had a nanny who did all of that. Mother was mostly interested in keeping up appearances.

CH 35 – DANIELLE
Boarding School

When Jordan turned twelve, he was sent away to a school in Bradenton, Florida called IMG Academy Boarding School. Even though we weren't that close, I was surprised to see how much I missed him. I would be joining him the following year, though.

Our nanny had been replaced with a governess, a 60-year-old Englishwoman named Millicent. She took care of all of the household duties, which included me. With Father, Mother, and Jordan gone, I was really, really lonely.

So, I occupied myself with television, the internet and reading. Through books, I could escape to anywhere and experience passion, lust, love, hate, joy – all of my subdued and not yet-discovered emotions.

While on the internet when I was about twelve, I started chatting with this boy named Glenn. He told me he was sixteen. We spent countless hours talking and texting. He asked for some sexy pictures. I first sent him pictures of me in bikinis and eventually I started sending him selfies of my breasts. He would reciprocate with selfies of his chest, biceps and six-pack. And finally, dick flicks. We then started sexting.

All of this eventually led to us planning to meet. By this time, I had developed deep feelings for him. I shared with him some of the dynamics of my family – my deep affection for Father and how much he loved me back – his little princess; the pain of Mother not loving me and her jealousy; missing my brother and never seeing enough of Father. He, in turn, responded with his sad stories of rejection from his father and his hardworking mother who rarely had time for him and his two sisters. Yes, we shared a common bond and I was looking forward to actually meeting him.

That day finally arrived. It was a Friday morning. We both were ditching school and had called the attendance offices, disguising our voices, alerting them of our absence. I googled Metro bus and got the proper bus route to Roxbury Park where we were scheduled to meet.

Dismounting the bus and running across the parking lot into the park, anticipating finally coming face to face with my new love, I was startled to see (you'd never guess) – Father! I almost fainted from shock.

What happened was that old lady Millicent had snooped around and heard my conversation with Glenn and passed it on to my father. And I thought she paid no attention to me. Wow! Well, I guess that showed she did care and — even more importantly — Father cared. Even with his busy schedule and the day off intended for relaxing, he was more interested in protecting me. I couldn't be angry at old lady Millicent and, most certainly, not Father.

Even though that was a fuzzy-feeling-kinda-moment, I wasn't prepared for what happened next. Father drove me home – silent – all the way. I'd never seen him that angry. Well, to be truthful – I'd never done anything other than not cleaning my room that upset him. After parking the car in the garage, we entered through the kitchen door. Mother just happened to be home at that exact time. Father ushered me into the living room and demanded that I sat and wait for him and Mother. We were going to have a meeting.

I couldn't believe that I was not going to be spending my last summer at home before going away to boarding school. Father and Mother both agreed that I couldn't be trusted and they were making plans for me to leave the following week — the last week of school!

I spent the next seven years at IMC Academy, going home only on holidays. I had a couple of girlfriends and a couple of boyfriends while there. I looked forward to returning home after graduation. Father had taken an early retirement and had promised me that we would be spending the entire summer before college, traveling and enjoying each other. Jordan had been going out with a girl he'd met at school for the past year and they were planning on doing their own thing. Mother – well, all she wanted to do was work on the fall fashions.

• • • • •

CH 36 - DANIELLE
Life Changes

I will never forget this day as long as I live. That day had finally arrived – graduation! I had spent seven arduous years here, away from my parents – especially Father. I donned my turquoise blue graduation robe and adjusted the matching cap, making sure the tassel was dangling on the right side.

I excitedly got in line in the order that was practiced, looking around for my parents. I saw Jordan grinning and waving wildly. I waved back, wondering why my parents weren't occupying the two reserved seats next to him.

The ceremony seemed to go on forever. Eventually, the seats reserved for my parents were filled. It was evident they weren't coming or they were awfully late. Panic started to rise inside me and I had to force myself to stay calm. Our names were called and we received our graduation diplomas. Finally, the ceremony that seemed to never end, ended.

I didn't have to look around too long before Jordan ran up to me, grabbing and hugging me profusely. He was crying. I knew he was happy but not *that* happy. After all, he had graduated a year earlier and he hadn't cried. My parents still hadn't arrived. I sensed something was wrong.

I soon found out. Sobbing, Jordan broke the devastating news. Our parents were involved in a fiery automobile accident. A big semi-truck had side-swiped them, sending them into a tailspin and over the edge of a cliff. They both were killed instantly.

•   •   •   •   •

CH 37 – DANIELLE
The Will

Life after death. Is there such a thing? After my parents' death, I was left numb. I felt like the walking dead. I didn't know what to do. All my plans were as dead as my parents. What was I going to do now?

I was consumed with making funeral plans. It had to be grand and classy — just like Mother would have liked. Millicent was an unforeseen source of strength. She helped me pick out the coffins and the clothing for the burials. Jordan didn't want to have anything to do with any of it. So, Millicent also helped me with the obituaries, the priest and the order of service. The scheduled day of the funeral services came and went as planned.

My parents' lawyer came by the next day to read the will. The inheritance was divided equally between my brother and me — the mini-mansion, the French chalet in Quebec, Mother's lucrative fashion design business and thirty million dollars in stocks, bonds, and money. We were instant millionaires and not prepared for the responsibilities. I decided to take that year off from college.

Jordan left the following Sunday, leaving me totally alone again. Millicent would continue to live and work at the mini-mansion. I needed her now more than ever. She had become more than a governess. She had become my friend and confidant.

The following Friday, a week after the funeral, I decided that I needed to get out of the house, so I did a search for a singles bar to go drinking and dancing. I finally settled on the one called *Catch Up*. It had a five-star rating, with great reviews.

It took me almost an hour trying to decide what to wear. I settled on one of my tight-fitting, little black mini-dresses, clipped on two rolls of extensions, and put on my make-up, applying extra mascara. I called for an Uber and off I went.

•　　•　　•　　•　　•

CH 38 - DANIELLE
My Daniel

I had to stand in the long line for only a few minutes before the bouncer allowed me in. I nervously glanced around the crowded room before I was lucky enough to find an empty seat at the bar. I ordered my signature drink – an apple martini. I quickly downed two of them, trying to get my buzz on. I was successful. The guy seated next to me offered to buy me another, hoping to get lucky. I was in no condition to refuse, so I accepted.

The next morning, I woke up with a splitting headache. I felt nauseous and bolted to the bathroom, making it just in time before throwing up everything in my gut. I can't ever remember being that sick. I didn't remember how or when I got home. All I know is that I was fully dressed, shy of my high heels, lying across my bed.

Millicent heard me throwing up and brought me some green tea, which helped a little. When I started feeling a little better, I looked on my night stand and found a note that read: *You got really sauced and the guy next to you was trying to take advantage of you, so I let you into my office until I got off. I'm the bartender. I found your address in your wallet and took you home and put you to bed. You can call and thank me at 310-555-6899. Daniel*

Oh wow! I was so embarrassed. I have no idea what I did or what I said. But I was grateful he saved me from a potentially bad situation. I called to thank him and the rest is history.

Daniel and I immediately hit it off. He was a gentleman, like Father. He was also tall like him. He was attentive and protective like Father. His kisses were delicious and sensual. We dated for a month before I lost my virginity to him. He couldn't believe it was my first time. Bells didn't go off or anything like that – it was just a good, good feeling.

I was happy. Daniel was my soul mate. We had the same name – his was the male version. We enjoyed a whirlwind relationship. Three months in, I decided he should move out of his small apartment and into my mini-mansion. Daniel agreed, only if I allowed him to be the bread-winner. Of course, I agreed.

I wanted him to quit his bartending job so he could spend more time with me and not be tempted by the myriad of beautiful single ladies looking for a good man. Of course being the man he was, he refused, but tried to assuage my fears by inviting me to the club anytime, telling me that there was no other woman for Daniel but Danielle.

●　　●　　●　　●　　●

CH 39 – DANIELLE
Losing My Baby

Six months into our relationship, I found out I was pregnant. Daniel and Millicent were thrilled. We celebrated with me drinking my last glass of wine for the next eight months. I immediately started planning for our new baby. It was too soon to know the sex, but that didn't stop me from shopping. I could buy yellow clothing and baby furniture.

I was well into my first trimester when I started feeling sharp stomach pains. This persisted for a couple of days, becoming increasingly worse. Daniel took me to the doctor and after a series of tests, it was determined that I was in the middle of a miscarriage. We were crushed! Why do I lose everything I love? I screamed out angrily to God.

After that, I fell into a deep depression. I experienced all of the signs: lack of interest in activities (including sex), sleepless nights, loss of appetite, trouble concentrating, feeling guilty and blaming myself. I even had thoughts of suicide. I was a total mess!

Daniel tried everything within his power to pull me out of my deep hole of depression, but to no avail. After a while, he stopped trying and I noticed that he started coming in later and later. He was drinking more than usual. One night, I smelled a woman's perfume on him. When questioned about it, he brushed it off saying that he always hugs his special patrons – men and women alike.

About a year into our relationship, Daniel came to me with a look on his face that I'd never seen before. "Sit down, honey, I have something to tell you".

I could feel the terror rising up in my throat. I sat as commanded, waiting nervously to hear what he was about to say. "I'm leaving you" was my first thought.

He cleared his throat and the words that came from his mouth made me want to throw up. "I have gotten another woman pregnant and in six months, we will be having a baby girl. I'm sorry, hon, but after you lost our baby, I lost you. I had no other choice but to seek out the company of another woman. Please forgive me, babe. Tania is her name. This will be her first baby and she's determined to keep it. I'll have to be there for the baby. I'm not in love with Tania. I love you. I just made a mistake. Please, please can you forgive me?"

After I regained my voice, I said quietly, "I'm going to have to think about this", left the room and fell on my bed, dissolving in body-wracking tears. I didn't speak to him until the next morning. "Daniel, I've thought about everything I've done and everything you've said and I'm sorry for pushing you away. I love and forgive you. We're going to work through this." We kissed, sealing our commitment.

•   •   •   •   •

CH 40 – DANIELLE
Jealousy Kills

I can say beyond a shadow of a doubt that getting through the next six months was no easy task. When Daniel would accompany Tania to the doctor for her prenatal care, twinges of jealousy would zing through my body like poison arrows. I had lost my baby and now I was losing my man.

That dreaded day finally came. We were jolted awake at 3:00 a.m. with his phone ringing. He sleepily answered it but quickly came alive after hearing the good news. The baby is coming! All I heard was, "The British are coming!" I don't know why. I just did.

After he jumped into his clothes and ran out the door, I tried to go back to sleep, but couldn't. I finally dragged my tired, sleep-deprived body from our California King bed and went into the kitchen to make coffee. "He didn't even kiss me good-bye" kept repeating itself over and over in my head.

Three hours later, my phone rang. It was Daniel, of course, telling me the good news. The baby girl weighed in at 7 lbs. 4 oz and she was beautiful and healthy. I tried to sound excited, but failed miserably.

•   •   •   •   •

Fast-forward six months. Little Penelope (I hated that name. I don't know why anyone would name their child that) is the apple of Daniel's eye. He and Tania shared joint custody and Penelope spent most weekends at our house. I was cordial to Tania, but secretly, I hated the bitch. She was the reason Daniel and I no longer had a good relationship. I hated her because she was able to give my man something I could not – a beautiful baby girl.

I resented all of the attention Daniel showered on Penelope. I don't know if he sensed my resentment or not; he never asked me to change her diaper or feed her. He took great pleasure in doing it all himself.

It's Penelope's first birthday! Millicent was scurrying about decorating the house and cooking, preparing for little Penelope's birthday dinner. Daniel had fed her and she was quietly sleeping in the crib that we had bought for our deceased child.

Millicent's car was being repaired, so she asked Daniel to drive her to pick up the birthday cake. He agreed.

He made sure Penelope was asleep and assured me they'd be back before she awakened.

The car had just exited our block-long driveway when Penelope woke up, looking for her daddy. When she found out he wasn't there, she started screaming at the top of her lungs. I tried everything I could to quiet her, but nothing worked. Her screaming was giving me an excruciating head-ache.

I covered her mouth to quiet her. That helped a lot. She stopped flailing her arms and legs and relaxed. Thank God, she was quiet. But then I realized that she had gone limp. I panicked and checked her pulse. There was none. I tried to resuscitate her, but to no avail. I then called 911.

The paramedics were there in less than five minutes! They used that machine that's supposed to jump-start your heart, but it didn't work. They finally put her on a giant gurney and drove away. As luck would have it, Daniel and Millicent were returning and ran into them. They were instructed to follow them to the hospital. I prayed for a miracle but it didn't happen.

• • • • •

Four hours later — just two hours before the scheduled birthday party, two police detectives knocked on my door. I was arrested and charged with second degree murder. I pleaded guilty, deciding not to go trial and was given a twenty-year sentence. I was 21 and with good behavior, I could be out by the time I'm 36.

I knew everyone hated me. The news painted me out to be a monster. My brother couldn't believe what I'd done, but didn't turn his back on me. He and Millicent were the only ones who would be coming to visit me. I knew Daniel didn't want to have anything to do with me. And of course, Tania hated my guts and was angry that I didn't get the death penalty.

• • • • •

CH 41 – DANIELLE
Redemption

I have been incarcerated for fourteen years now. I will be going before the parole board in two more years. I was lucky enough to get a job working in the prison library. Reading has always been my passion and when I'm not working, even when I'm working, you will find my head stuck in a book.

I've taken all of the self-help courses and workshops the prison offered. I was able to get a bachelor's degree in Psychology and certificates in drug and alcohol counseling and anger management. When I get out, I will be employable — even with a prison record.

My brother took over the conservatorship of all our property and finances, so I will have a place to stay when I get out.

•   •   •   •   •

I signed up for the Justice Reform Symposiums and was excited when I was chosen to participate in seminars and workshops to promote healing between victims and murderers.

I met Bettye at one of the symposiums, along with three fellow murderers, three victims, a D.A. and a social worker – nine people in our circle. We all shared our stories and cried tears of remorse, regret, and forgiveness. It was one of the most powerful and soul-freeing experience of my life. When Bettye stroked my face, told me how beautiful I was and hugged me, I couldn't hold back the tears. It had been such a long time since I'd received such love from anyone other than my brother and Millicent.

I finally got the courage to write to Daniel and Tania. I worked on this one-page letter for four months. The next time Jordan and Millicent come to visit, I will give it to them to take to them.

• • • • •

Dear Daniel and Tania:

I have been imprisoned for fourteen years and will be going before the parole board in about two years. I never got the chance to tell you both how truly sorry I am for taking your daughter's life. I swear, it wasn't intentional. She wouldn't stop crying for her dad and I tried to quiet her. I covered her mouth for too long and she stopped breathing.

I will regret what I did for the rest of my life. I think about Penelope every day. I heard you guys got married and had another little girl. Congratulations! I hope you are happy enough now to forgive me. Although another baby and more kids will never take the place of little Penelope, I wish you peace and everlasting love.

Sincerely,

Danielle Donovan

Ch. 42

ACE SCORE EVALUATIONS

U nlike psychology, the science of math is predict-
able. You know for a fact that when you add two
plus two, it will always compute to four; 10 X 100 will
always total 1,000, no matter where you are.

In science there are undeniable laws such as the laws
of physics which states that two objects cannot occupy
the same space at the same time except in the case of
electromagnetic waves. Another familiar scientific law
and also a much popular saying is, "What goes up must
come down". Jealous haters use that one a lot.

The science of psychology is unpredictable. It's like
taking a handful of marbles and tossing them in the air
and betting on the order in which they'd hit the ground.
That's ACEs for you. Cheryl had an ACE score of 9, yet
she joined the ranks of overcomers, thus proving that a
person's early childhood adversities does not always de-

fine them or relegate them to a lifetime of drug, alcohol abuse, and crime.

Take for example, Rita. Before I read Rita's story, I was convinced that she had been wronged by the amount of time she had to do. She had told us that she had been beaten several times and had called 911. She told us that her boyfriend's abuse often landed her in the emergency room. She told us that the prosecutors didn't even consider those past transgressions and the jurors were unaware and she was convicted.

After reading Rita's story, I was able to see why she received her 25 to life sentence. As you also read, she already had a rap sheet a mile long. She had been arrested for stabbing someone before that.

Her ACE score of 8, along with her father's abuse and her mother's lack of self-esteem and self-respect enabled her toward her dark pathway of life.

• • • • •

Three months later, I went to CIW to visit Rita and we played games and talked and ate expensive chicken wings and avocado from the vending machines. I enjoyed the three hours with her. We took pictures and finally terminated my first visitor's pass to CIW, assuring her that I would return.

Robin's ace score of 4 made her vulnerable to her molester because she was seeking to replace her father's love and affection. This grown man, her stepfather, took advantage of this little girl.

Robin was the cutest, chubby little girl, with an outgoing personality. She loved to dance and was pretty good at it. She had slimmed down just before starting kindergarten. She had a head full of the most thick, luxurious hair ever. May of her classmates envied her long, thick braids and, although they were jealous, they dared not mess with her because she was a known fighter.

Robin grew up and had an hour glass figure. Her chocolate skin was flawless. She received a lot of attention. She met and married the love of her life. She was happy and secure. She got pregnant and after that the weight piled on. She finally had gastric bypass surgery. She was back to that voluptuous, hour glass figure. She couldn't go anywhere without men and women ogling her. Successful and handsome men were hitting on her and she had to resist temptation. She was not comfortable with all that extra attention and a year later, I saw her and she had started putting the weight back on.

Often when people's stress response becomes activated, their biological systems are so over stimulated that they don't know what to make of it. In her case, she unconsciously started eating more. Perhaps if she gained her weight back, she wouldn't get so much attention and she could remain true to her vows.

It took several years for Robin to recognize this cause and effect of her weight gain and loss. She is still madly in love with her husband and her lovely teen-age daughter. Her past experiences have her keeping a watchful eye on her daughter. Her weight is no issue because she exercises and is healthy and, most of all, her husband loves every inch. She's a beautiful woman and receives appreciative glances everywhere she goes.

• • • • •

A person with four or more ACEs is two and a half times as likely to smoke, five and a half times as likely to be dependent on alcohol, and ten times as likely to use intravenous drug as a person with zero ACEs.

Robin's ACE score of 4 could have turned her into a sexual predator, she could have escaped through drugs and sexual deviancy, but she didn't. She's never smoked cigarettes or pot, never used intravenous drugs and only drank socially. Her strict Jehovah's Witness upbringing played a big part in her not succumbing to drugs and alcohol. Also, writing and sharing her story helped immensely. That's why I say that your past does not have to define you. Robin is a perfect example of that.

• • • • •

It's interesting to note that even though Cheryl had 9 of the 10 ACEs, she did not resort to the debauchery of drugs, alcohol, sex, or criminal activities. But her childhood adversities did not leave her unscarred. What happens to children's brains and bodies when they are exposed to a high ACE score?

Early childhood adversities effects are not only psychological, but physiological. Cheryl's deregulated stress response system is a resultant of the frequent and prolonged emotional and physical abuse. When the body senses danger, it discharges a chemical chain reaction aimed to protect itself. Neglect and violence disrupted Cheryl's organ systems and increased her risk for stress-related disease well into adulthood. Fight, flight, or freeze are the body's response mechanisms. Most of us are aware of the first two but freezing is another option.

When the stress response is activated too frequently, or the stressor too intense, the body can lose the ability to shut down the HPA and SAM axes. The simplest way to put it is the body's stress thermostat is broken. Instead of shutting off the supply of heat when a certain point is reached, it just keeps on blasting cortisol through your system.

That's exactly what happened to Cheryl. Her mom's abuse would elevate her cortisol thermostat and the repeated action over and over, used it up. Just like our cars, even with maintenance, everything breaks down and/or needs replacing and replenishing. Cheryl's mother's abuse exacerbated her body stress thermostat and over time, it was exhausted. That's why she has to stay hydrated and out of the sun as much as possible.

I was afforded the opportunity to visit Cheryl and Harriet recently when I went to visit my cousin, Wendell. Harriet's dad had built her a lovely three-bedroom home. It was cheerfully decorated in various turquoise tones, light blue and yellow. They were the proudest, happiest couple I'd seen in a while. I couldn't help shedding happy tears for Cheryl.

$\bullet$ $\bullet$ $\bullet$ $\bullet$ $\bullet$

You remember Carla. She had all 10 ACES! Her childhood experiences left her angry and bitter. That's why she'd fight at the drop of a hat. Carla was blessed with dedicated mentors who helped her to change her life.

There's no doubt that parents, a teacher, a friend or clergy can help change your life's direction. I ran across a book entitled, *The CEO, the Mentor & the Kid*. It showed the power of effective mentorship. This book charted a kid in prison's life change after meeting his lifelong mentor. Following in his footsteps, he became the CEO of his own company, just like his mentor.

Like the kid, Carla listened to her mentors – not always taking their advice, but continually growing in wisdom and experience. The love and appreciation these two have for their mentors manifests itself with their success. A direct quote from Carla: "I hate it when I disappoint Ms. Sweet".

I can see a bright and hopeful future for Kierra. She is blessed to have a supportive partner who was really down for her, no matter what. I'll never forget what Kierra said after sitting down with her Starbuck's coffee, "This is the first time I've ever had Starbuck's coffee. I've seen it advertised on TV and wondered what it tasted like".

I foresee a lot of Starbuck's coffee in Kierra's future and much, much more.

Danielle still has a long way to go. Because of the nature of her crime, she'd had to suffer unbearable abuse and even when she gets out, she must register as a child murderer. When I think of her, I always remember hugging and kissing her on the last day of the symposium and her words, "This is the first time I've been hugged like this in a long time. I feel loved."

I'm tearing up even while typing this. That was one of the saddest things I'd ever heard. She had shared with me that she couldn't remember her mother ever hugging or kissing her. Her dad was affectionate but she was never close with her brother. All of the affection she received was sexually-motivated. She had never known true love. I do so wish her love, peace and happiness when she finally gets out. She has my phone number, home and email address. She knows that I will always be just a phone call, a letter, or email away.

• • • • •

For you, the reader, if you have experienced any of these childhood adversities, the next chapter shares seven strategies for healing from PTSD (post-traumatic stress disorders) which I re-named, *Redemption Strategies*. The program was originally designed for secondary school children, but it has been used in the *Halfway Home* & the *Free 4 Lyfe* re-entry programs for ex-offenders.

• • • • •

Ch 43—
REDEMPTION STRATEGIES

Cry it Out

Webster defines **redemption** as the action of saving or being saved from sin, error, or evil. Another definition for redemption is the action of regaining possession of something in exchange for payment or clearing a debt.

Now that you've computed your ACE score and you know what you're working with, what will be your strategies for your redemption? The more acrimonious childhood experiences oftentimes manifest themselves through alcohol and substance abuse, cyclical violence, incarceration and mental health problems. But for most people, childhood trauma is simply something that you've tried to forget.

But every suppression of emotions and feelings eventually rises up, manifesting itself through broken relationships, health problems, alcohol and drug abuse. Post-Traumatic Stress Disorder is a stark reality in today's society. But people who are smart and strong with great support systems are able to rise above the past and triumph through the sheer force of their own will and resilience.

The problem with PTSD is that it becomes entrenched. The stress response is caught in the past, stuck on repeat with the body remembering too much. There's a plethora of organizations that you can contact for support and resources. Just Google.

In my book, *Survivor to Thriver*, there are seven strategies for healing which I incorporated into my *Write to Heal* Program for people suffering with PTSD. These strategies accelerated my journey toward my healing. I will share them with you, with hopes of your healing from your adverse childhood experiences.

> **Cry it Out** – *You will speak silently in the language of tears as your heart seeks to understand what it cannot.*
>
> Susan Squellati Florence

Whenever I reflect on our circle at the Justice Reform Symposium, I see a river of tears. Kierra, the group leader, shed the most. Her remorse and pain for murdering Mr. Kim was truly from her heart and soul. We, the victims, shed tears for the loss of our loved ones and they, the murderers shed tears of regret for their own crime and tears of sorrow for us.

I heard this saying years ago, "Pain is hardest for the strong". After I lost my son, people would comment about how strong I was, about how well I was holding up. It reminded me of a book entitled *I'm Dancing as Fast as I Can* but the sad truth was that I felt broken and weak, harboring that painful hole in my chest. I rarely cried in public but, boy, when I was alone, especially riding in my car, I would turn into a crying fool.

There's this song, *Big Girl's Don't Cry* by Frankie Valli and the Four Seasons that is most assuredly a lie. I feel sorry for little boys who are told that same lie.

The million-dollar question is when is it a good time to cry. The answer is, whenever you feel sad enough to cry. Don't suppress it. Cry it out. Allow yourself to get past that sad feeling by shedding tears or even bawling. Whenever I'm feeling really sad, I let the tears flow, dry my face, knowing that *this too shall pass*. Trying to ignore the sadness does you no good. You must go with the flow of your emotions.

Crying is a uniquely human trait. I'm willing to bet you've never seen your dog or cat cry. The situations that make us cry are often the ones we remember most. It shows we are sensitive to things we encounter in our lives and, in that way, it is important for survival. Spilling tears is something we all need to stay healthy.

Strong emotions cause our brains to release chemicals that indirectly lead to teary eyes. A flow of tears shoots up the level of endorphins, natural chemicals within the body, providing a sense of well-being and **relieving stress**, but also they release toxins — making us healthier, according to **Dr. William Frey II**, a neurologist at the **University of Minnesota**.

The physical act of crying is rooted in psychological **depression**. When bad things happen and people don't cry, either that person is trying to avoid this depression or he or she may have a disease associated with tears that can prevent them.

Let's not forget that tears are shed not only for sadness, but there are happy tears. I've shed more happy tears over my lifetime than sad tears, I'm grateful and blessed to say.

•　　•　　•　　•　　•

Ch 44
REDEMPTION STRATEGIES

2. Talk it Out

Talking it out in our circle was therapeutic for everyone involved. Everyone in the group was open and honest, sharing their stories and their feelings. We left the first session feeling lighter having gotten so much off our chests.

When should you talk about your problems and anxieties? It's a good idea to talk it out if you are feeling unclear and the lack of clarity is making you feel anxious, down or uninspired. When being alone is no longer helping your peace of mind, you should find someone to talk to.

It can help to talk to someone you trust; it could help you sort through your problem or see your situation more clearly. It can help you look at your problem in a different way and can release built-up tension and gain new insight into whatever it is that's causing you a problem. Talking it out helps you to make better decisions. It can help you realize that you are not alone. SO, DON'T KEEP YOUR PROBLEMS TO YOURSELF.

Talking to the right person can help you feel better. It is important to figure out who the best person is to talk to. If you feel unsafe or feel your privacy will be compromised, then perhaps a counselor or other professional who specializes in talking to people would be a good choice. Talking to someone else also helps you to become a better listener, hopefully.

There are 24-hour help lines, school counselors in high school or college, and there are trusted loved ones and friends. Use these resources whenever you feel the need.

What should you talk about? You can talk about your childhood, your pain or tragedy in your life. Never keep these emotions bottled up inside; it is destructive locked inside.

You can talk about your aspirations, dreams, and hopes for a brighter future. Always find someone who wants to inspire you to be better and greater. Stay clear of jealous people and haters. Talk about your problems and discuss possible solutions. Oftentimes another person can see through your solutions better than you can.

You know, of course, that you can't talk to just anyone. If someone makes you feel you are a bother when you need to talk, then this is simply not the right person. Find someone who cares about your plight. As before-mentioned, this doesn't have to be a personal friend; it can be one of many professionals.

Your problems matter to you and if there is a problem, then there must be a source to help remedy it. You are no bother because you need to talk it out. Just find the right person or the right professional so you can talk it out – another avenue toward your healing.

•   •   •   •   •

Ch 45
REDEMPTION STRATEGIES

3. Write it Out

Take a chunk of your heart and spread it over some paper. It goes, oh, such a long way.

James T. Mangan

That's exactly what Cheryl did. Part of her healing came about through her journaling and writing her book. A lot of my healing came about through my journaling and writing my books also.

Writing it out is the third of the seven redemption strategies. You have cried a river of tears. You have clenched your fists in anger and cursed God and His entire crew. You have talked it out with friends, psychiatrists, and even complete strangers. Doing all of the above can help you get back on the freeway of recovery, but you still need to do more.

When you write it out it helps you ride it out because writing is excellent practice in clear thinking. Taking a book and notepad with you helps to keep your mind occupied while waiting for appointments at the doctor's office and other duties. Writing helped get me through my life's worst experience – the death of my son. My morning routine of typing my diary was part of my therapy. Working on my book gave me something to do every morning and gave me a sense of purpose.

Father Arnold Pangrazzi said, "The road to recovery from pain is to take time to do things that will enable us to give a renewed meaning to our lives. That's when our journey through grief and pain becomes a journey of discovering ourselves, our potential, and our resources in the encounter with life. That's when we become BETTER PEOPLE rather than BITTER PEOPLE".

Allow yourself to focus on your adverse childhood experiences by writing it out. Let time work your pain by staying active. Find some place to volunteer; create a memory book or video; plant a garden; do something you always wanted to do; or create and/or support a cause. Robin, Rita, Kierra, Cheryl and I all used writing as a strategy to help with our healing. Robin and Cheryl wrote books, like I did.

Why write it out? You write because expressing emotions has healing powers. The excessive holding back of thoughts, feelings, and behaviors can place you at risk for both major and minor diseases. Writing about your pain is more than simply a catharsis or venting; translating your painful events into language can affect your brain and immune functions. Writing provides a means to externalize traumatic experiences and therefore render them less overwhelming

When you "write it out" the upsetting experience is repeatedly confronted; the emotional reactivity you feel as you assess its meaning and impact is weakened. Once organized through writing it out, traumatic events become smaller and smaller and therefore easier to deal with.

Just like "talking it out," writing helps to express your feelings and to release built-up tensions so you can make better decisions.

Writing about your pain helps you to move beyond trauma because the process of writing about it provides a means for the experience to become psychologically complete. Writing it out can help you heal. And who knows, it could turn into a published book.

How often and how long should you write? Go easy on yourself. If the pain is too intense, take a break. Go for a walk. Go to a baseball game or to a party. Have coffee with a friend. Seek the people and activities that make you feel most secure. Balance these breaks with the writing. But don't use this to avoid the memories. Use it to help you keep going.

If you're really struggling, consider professional help. Talking with a counselor or a trusted friend can help you open up to start healing and writing; it can actually strengthen your writing. If it helps you recognize things at a deeper level, then you'll be all the more truthful and real as you write.

What should you write about? Write about your pain. It is inside you and if you don't bring it out and face it head on, it will quietly and destructively control you. You won't know why you're angry; you won't know why you can't sleep; you won't know why you're not at peace.

To write the pain, you have to revisit it. But sometimes those blocks and protections you've built are hard to break down. Try some prompts to bring back the emotions. Look at old pictures from that time period. Listen to music — even if a song isn't directly connected, its style and tones can speak to the deep feelings within you. Keep your notebook with you always, ready to catch whatever may come.

How should you write it out? Grab your sheet of paper, laptop, or your journal. Go where you're comfortable and distraction-free. Set aside a defined period of time - about 30 minutes or an hour. Devote that time to a particular challenging memory. Just sit and face it.

Start small. Don't try to write everything about your childhood or tragedy. Write that one specific scene. Don't write that you were always angry at your brother. Write about that one fight - you know the one.

What did you see and smell? What were you wearing? What did you say? Give specific details, all the bits and pieces. Don't worry about how it comes out or what you'll do with it later. Just write it out. Maybe in your first session, you won't write a word. Or maybe you'll write 15 pages. It doesn't matter. Do it, and then set another time to do it again.

•　　•　　•　　•　　•

Ch 46
REDEMPTION STRATEGIES

4. Forgive it Out

Forgiving David Cunningham, the man who murdered my son, was one of the hardest things I've ever done in my entire life. I hated whoever had anything to do with Jason's murder. It wasn't until the detectives matched the cigarette butt at the crime scene with his water glass at a restaurant, was he finally arrested. He had gotten "saved", married and had a 3-year-old daughter. He pleaded guilty and was sent to prison without my ever going to court. I don't know what he looks like, to this day. I had to know what happened, so I wrote him a letter.

•　　•　　•　　•　　•

Dear David Cunningham:

I'm sure you're surprised to hear from me, the mother of Jason Sweet. When you murdered my son, my entire world was turned upside down. He was 18, my only son, in college and working – doing what he was supposed to be doing.

For more than a year, even with writing my book, *Survivor to Thriver: A Mother's Journey Toward Peace After Her Son's Murder*, every single morning I'd wake up angry that I woke up because I didn't want to face the pain of yet another day.

Your actions changed many, many lives. I just would like to know if you really realize what you did – the pain and agony you caused!? Do you regret what you did – not just because you got caught? Just tell me how does that affect your soul? Do you even remember his face? Here it is, just in case you don't.

I'm trying my best to forgive you, but I need to hear what you have to say. Please, please write me back.

Bettye Sweet

•　　•　　•　　•　　•

A week later, I received an 8-page legal-size letter from David. He told me his account of the murder. He said that after he shot Jason, he immediately left to return home in Texas. Reading his first letter left me with many questions. I felt David was sorry, but for what? For murdering my son or for getting caught? I didn't feel that he was taking full responsibility for his actions. He was blaming Wink and the "mis-firing" gun.

We exchanged several letters the first three or four years until he wrote a letter that really pissed me off and I told him to stop writing me and I stopped writing him for five years.

After I went to the women's prison, I wrote an article that was published in the San Quinten Prison, not knowing that it went to hundreds of other prisons also. I also wrote a letter to David after we both had five years to think and grow. He responded with the following letter.

•　　•　　•　　•　　•

Hey Ms. Sweet!

What up Queen!? I got too much to tell you. I don't know where to start.

OK, so around the time we lost contact, I just started looking into a new law that passed called SB1437 which changes the definition of the law I was convicted under. I thought this might be away to get the life taken off my sentence. I only qualified for this relief because I took a plea deal. I submitted the petition and was appointed an attorney. For almost five months I had not heard from him, then yesterday, Sept. 16th, I got a letter from him.

He was telling me this law is for the non-shooter, and since the day I turned myself in, I have taken responsibility for the shooting, I would have to spin the story and place the gun in someone else's hand. All I want is to get home to my daughter and my dad. Then on the other hand, I have you and Jason's honor. I couldn't live with myself if I spun the story and it caused you to think I lost sight of the hurt I had caused.

For about an hour, I was walking back and forth in the day room with tears in my eyes because I saw a small chance of getting home but I'd have to lie to get there. Then someone walked up to me and handed me the San Quentin Newspaper. I sat down and thumbed through it and came across you and

Jason's picture and the article you wrote! I was like, what the f#ck! I read your beautiful words and I knew it was God telling me he was in control and you and Jason means more than a lie.

So, I chose to write my lawyer and say if I can't get relief without turning my back on the truth.

THEN as I'm writing him, your letter just slid under my door. I SWEAR GOD IS TALKING! I love you Queen. I love you so much! Anyways, I'm full of emotions right now. I can't write any more. I'll write you soon. And I still want that hug and visit from you, so I can truly apologize. Write back.

Love,

David

September 18, 2019

Hey Queen, I'm back. I had to cut that letter short because it was too emotional for me because it was the first time in years that I felt God moving in my life. I lost my faith these last few years because of everything that has happened in my life. Some people are gangsters that take lives and have no remorse, and here I am – someone that made a decision to participate in a robbery and that one choice shattered so many lives. In my mind I felt God should have prevented the gun from mis-firing. For a long time, I overlooked the decisions I made that lead to that instant the gun went off. I only focused on the fact that it was really an accident.

Then, about five years ago, I realized that yes, the gun going off was unintentional, but everything leading up to that point was all my choice. I chose to come to Cali. I chose to go on a stick-up. I CHOSE to point a loaded gun at Jason, so it was all my doing. God didn't do anything! That's when I accepted my incarceration and I deserved to be punished.

But He was still allowing my relationship with my wife to deteriorate and make my contact with my daughter – un-existent. So that caused another spiritual battle. Queen, it was getting more and more difficult to still trust in God. Even right now I feel bad talking about my issues with a person (you) that has lost so much more – more than I can even imagine, like, "Nigga you got the nerve to talk about your pain"....and that's the voice that always brings *me back to focus on you and your strength which leads me to seeing God is real!*

When I say I love you Bettye Sweet, it's not to be cute or flatter you – it's the absolute truth because in those times when I questioned God's existence, He ALWAYS uses you to remind me He does! How could I not love someone who is the only reason I still believe in my Creator! THAT'S SOME REAL SHIT (excuse my language). I LOVE YOU!!

Like reading your letter about getting back with your ex-husband gives me hope about my relationship. You finding a purpose after the worst event in your life gives me hope. August 31ˢᵗ I just turned 39. I'm not a kid no more – I'm a grown-ass man and if it wasn't for going through this, I'd still be a boy in my mind!

Anyways, let me get this out to you. "Til we meet, QUEEN. ONE LOVE. I love you!
David

Last year, I wrote a letter to Governor Newsome regarding his release.

• • • • •

Dear Governor Newsom:

There's no doubt in my mind that this letter is unprecedented. I am writing this letter on behalf of David Cunningham, the young man who murdered my 18-year-old son, Jason Sweet-Williams, 14 years ago on December 17, 2004, a week before Christmas. Jason was my only son and the most precious young man ever!

David was given a sentence of 25 years to life, I think. He has been incarcerated for about 10 years. I reached out to him because I needed to know what happened since he had decided to plead guilty and be sentenced. Since then we have exchanged count-less letters. I'm enclosing his latest.

The reason for this letter is to request that when Cunningham goes before the parole board in the next five or six years that I be notified of the hearing. His father is ailing and his daughter needs to know her father. He left when she was three. I know, I know, this sounds crazy!

We are all given choices. My choices were to be bitter and unforgiving or to forgive and thrive.

Many of my friends think I'm crazy, but neither choice will bring Jason back so I chose to forgive which was healing for both me and David. He is remorseful and seriously sorry. How many times have we done things that we wish we hadn't?

Even you, I remember when you were busted for sleeping with your campaign manager's wife. I know that was a challenging period but, in the end, you were forgiven and given a second chance with your career and marriage. Because of the incredible power of forgiveness, you now have a thriving marriage and you're the governor of California!

As you already know — things happen for a reason. Because of Jason's death, I wrote my fourth book, Survivor to Thriver – A Mother's Journey Toward Peace After Her Son's Murder; a Write to Heal PTSD program for secondary school children; Change Gang, an Anti-bullying program for elementary and middle schoolers; Halfway Home, a re-entry program for ex-offenders. Because Jason died, I have a charter school, Home Sweet Home YouthBuild for the past 9 years, empowering more than a thousand youth – 16-25.

I know you receive thousands of letters and requests. I hope this one reaches you. I look forward to an expeditious response.

•　　•　　•　　•　　•

I have yet to receive a response from him or his office. I also wrote letters to Dr. Phil, Van Jones, and Steve Harvey asking them to film my first meeting with David. Haven't heard from them either. I'm nervous, but anxious to actually come face to face with my son's murderer. He says he wants to look me in my eyes, hug me and tell me again how truly sorry he is. I'm looking forward to that.

Forgiveness is a bad word to our penal and judicial system. You read how David tried to make contact with me, but it wasn't allowed. Had it not been for my persistence, we would not have had any communication until his parole hearing.

One of the things I learned at the justice symposium was that inmates are instructed not to make eye contact with the victim's family during court proceedings or parole hearings. I, and the other victims were totally unaware of this, thinking they didn't because they were ashamed, embarrassed, or just blatantly disrespectful.

In many cases, such as with the four ladies in our circle, after a certain point they yearned to make atonement. They yearned to be forgiven. But within our punitive systems, it's unlikely that will happen. Through the workshops and symposiums my ladies got creative and found a way to connect with their victim's family and wrote letters.

Who knows how the recipients will respond? The key factor is that my ladies put forth the effort. I hope and pray that each of the victim's family members can find it in their hearts to forgive these ladies — the ones who ended the lives of their loved ones. I also pray when their parole hearings come up the victim's family members won't block their early release. Forgiving is hard, but trust me, they can get to that point. It may take a while. It took me five years.

•　　•　　•　　•　　•

Cheryl did not have to beg for forgiveness because she was the innocent victim. She could have harbored hate for her mother but used instead, her gift of writing and forgiving to find redemption. She loved her mom enough to recognize that she had mental problems so she never blamed her. Forgiving was intrinsic in Cheryl's soul. Her book, POF (Power of Forgiveness — not to be confused with Plenty of Fish which should be POC – Plenty of Catfish) exemplified that.

• • • • •

For those of you who have weathered the storm of your adverse childhood experiences, your redemption will only be found through forgiving your parents and/or caregivers such as foster parents and relatives. It does no one any good by casting blame and finger-pointing. It is counterproductive and impedes healing and growth. If you can forgive the pain, the abuse, the neglect and the abandonment, the molestation, you will discover what the Higher Power has experienced: what you give to another, you give to yourself.

All things that proceed from you return to you. Sevenfold. So, there is no need to worry about what you are going to get back. There is only a need to worry about what you are going to give out. Life is about creating the highest quality of giving, not the highest quality of getting because forgiving is living.

We begin by forgiving God or the fate we see ruling the universe. We must forgive parents, relatives and friends for abandoning us in our time of need. Cheryl, Kierra, Carla, Robin, Danielle, Rita and I — we all had to embrace forgiveness in order to heal. Kierra, Carla,

Rita, and Danielle had to work on forgiving themselves. Let us heed the quiet message heard so softly in that maelstrom of the spirit: Forgive, forgive until forever. After that, put your pain aside and help someone, which brings us to the next strategy for healing.

•　　•　　•　　•　　•

Ch 47

REDEMPTION STRATEGIES

5. Forget You, Help Someone

You cannot do a kindness too soon, for you never know how soon it will be too late.

Ralph Waldo Emerson

Because we serve the Higher Power through serving others, I found that by helping other grief-stricken parents, my pain was lessened. Through my multitude of friends, I learned the importance of reaching out to help as they had reached out to me during my most crucial time.

Be a giver and you will discover the deepest secret of getting is in the giving. The more you give, the more you will have. The spiritual world is an upside-down world. You must give to get. My father used to say, *"If you have a closed fist, nothing can go out and nothing can get in."*

My father derived a lot of joy from giving, like I do. If you give someone a helping hand without having an ulterior motive, you will eventually be repaid. More than likely, it won't come from that person, but from someone or somewhere else.

The quickest way to heal is by getting involved in helping someone else or in a project. Keeping busy is one of the things that will help get your mind off your pain.

One of my most cherished and most practiced mottos is: *The pleasure of giving pleasure is the greatest pleasure of all.* Think back about making something, shopping, or planning a surprise party for someone. Those serotonins start to flow. Whenever you give to someone or make them happy, the receiver's serotonin rises. The serotonin of the giver rises also. Even the observer's serotonin rises and he also benefits from the mere observation of the act of kindness. One's immune system is also strengthened because of the serotonin.

President John F. Kennedy said, *"Ask not what your country can do for you, but what you can do for your country".* This kind of thinking is exactly what you need to help pull you out of the doldrums. Assisting others helps you to be thankful for your blessings.

• • • • •

Ch 48
REDEMPTION STRATEGIES

6. Praise, You Raise; Complain, Remain

It's not easy being grateful all the time. But it's when you feel least thankful that you are most in need of what gratitude can give you.

Oprah Winfrey Nov. 2004

"**S**ay thank you!" These are the words from Maya Angelou to Oprah Winfrey after Oprah called her blabbering and boohooing over the phone incoherently. When Oprah asked why, she was told "…because your faith is so strong that you don't doubt that whatever the problem, you'll get through it. You're saying thank you because you know that even in the eye of the storm, God has put a rainbow in the clouds. You're saying thank you because you know there's no problem created that can compare to the Creator of all things. Say thank you."

I discovered I could rise out of the dumpster by listing all of the things I had to be thankful for. I had a good running car; my health, no pain anywhere; a profession; a wonderful daughter; Jason's friends visiting — the longer I wrote, the happier I became.

Every day is a new day. Each day moves us a little further away from the pain of yesterday. Being thankful moves you from the negative to the positive. If you can thank God while you're going through the storm, you will be rewarded with peace and joy eventually.

Complaining does you no good. Complain and remain. My father used to say: *I complained because I had no shoes until I saw a man with no feet.* Be thankful for what you have and stop complaining about what you don't have.

When you are constantly dwelling on the negatives you bring not only yourself down, but others around you as well. It is impossible for you to be depressed if you are busy thanking God and appreciating the people who have shown you compassion, kindness and love.

Sending thank you notes to friends and relatives makes you feel good and makes the receiver feel good.

Remember: *In all things give thanks*. But most importantly, utilize the power of prayer and positive thinking.

•   •   •   •   •

Ch 49
REDEMPTION STRATEGIES

7. Prayer & Positive Thinking

It is the fire of suffering that brings forth the gold of Godliness.

Madame Guyon

We are not here by accident. Each of us is part of the divine plan of God. We, being the children of The Higher Power, bring enjoyment to Him and living to please Him is our main purpose in life. I always acknowledge God first, then I meditate while counting my blessings and thanking Him.

When you are living your life fully and with purpose, you are moving in the positive. We've all heard the saying that an idle mind is the devil's workshop. I once heard a comedian tell the story about the man who came running up to the Pope to tell him that Jesus was coming up the street. "What should I do?" he asked. The Pope retorted, "Look busy."

Your highest thought is a prayer, in a sense. That is why it is of the utmost importance to keep positive thoughts. When you are crying and thinking about your adverse childhood experiences, you can *change your mind* and switch to thinking of happy thoughts. Nobody said that it would be easy. But I am a living witness that it can be done.

Keep those thoughts positive. Think back to the good old days. Dwell on them. Make plans to be happy. Speak positive plans. Reject negative thoughts and negative people who put them there. Oftentimes, I don't watch the news because I want to stay positive. I watch sitcoms and game shows instead. I used to enjoy watching Ellen DeGeneres trying to dance. She loves it so much even though she knows she's not that good. Educational shows provide positive learning experiences and can open up your world to new experiences and new ideas.

Productive planning inspires hope. In Langston Hughes' *A Dream Deferred*, he talks about what happens when a dream is deferred. You cannot dry up like a raisin or stink with rot. You must take that dream and continue with it, no matter what. Because when one door closes, the Higher Power opens a window or another door. Where there is life, there is hope. And where there is hope, there is life.

Prayer changes things. The other day I was telling my friend Mary Ann that I get everything that I pray for unless I change my mind. It may not happen when I want it, but trust me, it's always on time. She laughingly agreed that I was right. She has been one of my best friends for over twenty years so she knows my desires, goals, and aspirations.

I hope that you too will become cognizant of the awesome power of God and the power of prayer. Prayer and positive thinking are synonymous. On several occasions I have run into old friends and they tell me that they have been thinking about me and praying for me. I'm always surprised and thankful for their positive thoughts.

Thoughts, emotions, and faith are pure energy in action. These energies never die. All thoughts congeal and like energy attracts like energy. When two or more people concentrate on the same energy (prayer, in this case), an incredible maze of energy is formed, creating an ever-changing pattern of unspeakable power and complexity.

All of these energies "sticking together," all of these positive thoughts and prayers from family and friends helps to form matter in the form of a more favorable reality. Their prayers mattered and although often I was unaware, they enabled me to be steadfast and helped me to begin my climb out of the depths of despair. Thoughts begin in the mind and heart and are communicated through the words that we speak. So, speak in the positive and for heaven's sake, watch your mouth.

• • • • •

Utilizing all of the seven strategies helped accelerate my healing and I found the peace and joy that I'd lost. Reading Dr. Harris' *The Deepest Well - Healing the Long-Term Effects of Childhood Adversity* helped me to put to rest many of my "whys".

Dr. Harris' interactive questionnaire/survey answered a lot of questions about why I do what I do and is now being used in clinics, hospitals and some schools. I recommend incorporating this survey for all intake applications — state and federal. Knowledge is power and this survey helps you to probe into your childhood with the hope of finding answers to your emotional and physical being.

I invite you to find out your ACE score by circling yes or no on the questionnaire. Complete the prompts at your convenience. Find a quiet time (preferably early morning), meditate and write your heart out.

EPILOGUE

Like the falling marbles, you could have an ACE score of only 1 and still fall prey to drug, alcohol addiction and criminal activities. My ACE score of 1 which was sexual molestation at the age of four drove me from man to man, sometimes women, never fully committing because I never wanted to be taken advantage of or hurt. I've had minor heartbreaks, including five divorces, but I am a survivor. Because I love myself, I never want to be the victim because being a victor feels so much better.

According to Dr. Harris, "Twenty years of medical research has shown that childhood adversity literally gets under our skin, changing people in ways that can endure in their bodies for decades. It can tip a child's developmental trajectory and affect physiology. It can trigger chronic inflammation and hormonal changes that can last a lifetime. It can alter the way DNA is read and how cells replicate, and it can dramatically increase the risk for heart disease, stroke, cancer, diabetes — even. Alzheimer's".

Children have faced childhood adversities, bullying, mental and physical abuse and challenges throughout history since the beginning of time, but most of them, like you, the reader, have transcended these adversities.

If you haven't gotten anything from this book other than my resounding message that your ACE score DOES NOT DEFINE YOU, my job will be done. Robin, Cheryl and Carla exemplify that. The other three victimized because they were victims. But, as you read, they fell down, made drastic mistakes and decisions and paid for them by doing time in prison. Through it all, their stories are of resilience, strength, faith, repentance, forgiveness – all of this leading to RE-DEMPTION.

No one ever said life would be easy and it certainly has been no bed of roses. On second thought — maybe life has been a bed of roses — complete with the thorns. The Universe has given us the gift of choice. You can cop out by letting your adversities define your choices or you can do like the ladies you've read about in this book and take those sour lemons and make lemon meringue pie. Children make lemon-aid. Grown-ass women make lemon meringue pie, which incidentally happens to be the title of my next book. Keep an ear and eye open for *How Sweet It Is – Turning Life's Sour Lemons into Lemon Meringue Pie.*

• • • • •

WHAT IS YOUR ACE SCORE?

Circle yes or no
   Prior to your 18th birthday:

1. Did a parent or other adult in the household **often** swear at you, insult you, put you down, or humiliate you?

    yes   no

    If yes, enter 1____

2. Did a parent or other adult **often** push, grab, slap, or throw something at you?

    yes   no

    If yes, enter 1____

3. Did an adult or someone at least five years older than you **ever** touch or fondle you or have you touch them OR attempt or have oral, anal, vaginal sex with you?

yes   no

If yes, enter 1____

4. Did you **often** feel unloved or felt you weren't important or special?

yes   no

If yes, enter 1____

5. Did you **often** feel that you didn't have enough to eat, had to wear dirty clothes and felt you had no one to protect you?

yes   no

If yes, enter 1____

6. Were parents ever separated or divorced?

yes   no

If yes, enter 1____

7. Was your mother or stepmother **often** pushed, hit, slapped,verbally abused, threatened?

yes   no

 If yes, enter 1____

8. Did you live with someone who was a **heavy** drinker, alcoholic, or drug user?

yes   no

If yes, enter 1____

9. Was a household member depressed, mentally ill, or attempted suicide?

yes   no

If yes, enter 1___

10.Did a household member go to jail?

yes   no

If yes, enter 1___

Now add up your number 1 answers.

Your ACE score___

How has your ACE score affected your teen-age, young adult, and later years in your life? How has your ACE score impacted your emotional, psychological and physiological self? Help yourself find the answers by completing the personal journal on the following page.

MY PERSONAL JOURNAL

I was born on _____ at _____ hospital.

I have ____ siblings ____ brothers and ____ sisters.

I was raised by my _____ because

_____

_____

_____

_____

_____

_____

_____

_____

My childhood memories:

_____

_____

_____

_____

_____

_____

Events that changed my life

_____

_____

_____

_____

_____

_____

_____

The most painful thing I've faced in my life was

_____

_____

_____

_____

_____

_____

_____

I wish

_____

_____

_____

_____

I regret

_____

_____

_____

_____

_____

_____

If I could change one thing, it would be

_____

_____

_____

_____

_____

_____

_____

I forgive _____ for

_____

_____

_____

_____

_____

_____

I forgive myself for

_____

_____

_____

_____

_____

The person(s) to whom I'd like to make amends are

_____

_____

_____

_____

I am thankful for

_____

_____

_____

_____

_____

_____

The strategy(ies) that I've found most useful on my road
to redemption

_____

_____

_____

_____

_____

_____

_____

I just want to add

_____

_____

_____

_____

_____

_____

_____

_____

• • • • •

About the Author

Bettye Sweet's first book, Growing Up L.A.Style: Byron, was written for inner-city school children looking for relevant reading material. The second book was written with Dr. Jefferson for teachers to help motivate students entitled, Differentiated Curriculum Strategies for ESL and Learning-Disabled Students. Her third book, Survivor to Thriver: A Mother's Journey Toward Peace After Her Son's Murder was a self-help book with seven strategies for healing. This fourth book is about her journey and the people she met after her son's death.

Sweet graduated from the University of Redlands and Union Institute. She received her master's of science degree in instructional leadership in curriculum and instruction from National University.

Sweet worked in the world of entertainment for many years before embracing the world of academia. She has also performed in the White House and on the Johnny Carson Show.

From 2010 to 2019 she was CEO/founder of Home Sweet Home YouthBuild, a charter school for "at-promise" youth, ages sixteen to twenty-five. Ms. Sweet resides in Los Angeles after the murder of her eighteen-year-old son, Jason. Sweet has four grandsons, thirteen great-grandchildren; and one great-great grandchild.